William Rushton is a television, stage and radio person as well as a renowned illustrator and cartoonist. Previous exploits in the book field include *Superpig*, *Pigsticking – A Joy For Life* and *Unarmed Gardening*.

THE
RELUCTANT
EURO

EUROPE ON $10,000,000 A DAY

Bloody Foreigners!

Rushton Versus Europe
★ William Rushton ★

Futura
Macdonald & Co
London & Sydney

A Futura Book

First published in Great Britain by
Queen Anne Press, Macdonald Futura Publishers in 1980

First Futura edition 1981
Reprinted 1982

Illustrations by William Rushton

ISBN 0 7088 2095 6

Printed and bound in Great Britain by
Hazell Watson & Viney Ltd, Aylesbury, Bucks

Futura Publications
A Division of
Macdonald & Co (Publishers) Ltd
Holywell House
Worship Street
London EC2A 2EN

CONTENTS

Introduction ——————————————— 6
Euro-History ——————————————— 9
Ins and Outs ——————————————— 28
France —————————————————— 42
West Germany ——————————————— 57
Belgium —————————————————— 62
Ireland —————————————————— 72
Italy ——————————————————— 77
Denmark ————————————————— 84
The Netherlands ——————————————— 88
Luxembourg ———————————————— 92
Euro-Diseases ——————————————— 94
The End ————————————————— 96

Introduction

There are those who may well say that this book is a little late, the horse having bolted and de Gaulle having been divided into three parts (for ease of burial, rumour has it). Had the book but appeared before the Great Wilson* Referendum, then it might have been relevant, pithy, topical yet, and have changed the course of British history as we know it.

My reply is that this seems as good a time as any. Having officially been a Euro-person for nigh on a decade, how come I have never felt less European in my life? Admittedly, I was Euro-persona non-starter from the off, but I've tried, God knows, to sway with the will of the people. What were the figures? Well, 67.2 per cent muttered 'Yes' quickly, or nodded furtively and hid their heads in buckets. Meanwhile 32.8 per cent, stout-hearted folk, cried 'No' in one strong, loud voice, sang 37 choruses of *Rule Britannia* and each downed a bottle of Coronation Stout in one patriotic gulp. Out of the window went Land, Hope and poor dear Gloria, who cared too deeply. That was that. Democracy, when it comes down to it, is one vote every five years that you invariably regret a fortnight later.

The issue was clear as a bell in my book.

Picture yourself at home, contentedly trepanning the wife with your Black and Decker or teaching the cat to bark at Arabs, when the phone goes. 'There's this super party', it shrills. 'Come at once. We've got this charming couple from Munich, he shaves his head and she's wonderfully Bavarian . . . a simply delightful French pair, she's a chiropodiste and he's with the *Comédie Française* . . . a madly gay Belgian root vegetable spokesman and his Walloon bride . . . and Guido, a really sweet Italian centre-back, who's brought his probation officer and a stretcher. Miss Holland is coming, too, if she can get through the door. She loves her food. And her manager's with her, though he'll probably have to stay in the garden. Then there are two Luxembourgers who are real delights . . . he owns the garage there . . . and two Guinnesses and a couple of pints of Carlsberg.'

Admit it, you'd make an excuse and stay away. Not even the added promise of some Portuguese sardine-salesmen's imminence, or the possible arrival of a chara-load of picadors from Madrid, would lure you. You warm for only a second when the opportunity of breaking plates over the heads of a Zorba-like formation dancing team from Piraeus presents itself, but there's no place, after all, like home.

Conversely, just when you're in the middle of the tricky bit with your power-tool and the cat has wagged its tail at a passing Persian, the phone rings again. Another binge. But this time it's a gang of Australian dentists on the razzle, plus roaring New Yorkers and weird San Franciscans, Indian gurus and a Jamaican dustbin band, bare-breasted Zulu chorines,

Harold Wilson, a former prime minister, best known for asking the nation to 'Give a year for Britain', and pissing off a month later.

lumberjacks and ice-hockey players from the land of maple leaf syrup – as well as some New Zealanders, but then into every life a little rain must fall. There will be red-hot vindaloos and ice-cold Resch's, Jack Daniels and proper hamburgers. Ha! You'd down tools in a trice and evict the scrofulous Tom Moggy: and they say civilisation is far from well. Apart from which, they all speak English.

That's all.

No, it isn't.

God knows (and did He not so plan it?) there's a motley enough bag of languages, accents, ethnic variations, local customs and rotten old folk-songs on these benighted islands, collected over a thousand years from invading or escaping Europeans, without looking round for more. The United Kingdom was an attempt to lump us all together under one head office in Westminster, the Brussels of its day, and look what happened to that.

It is highly ironical in my book, and my book it is, so highly ironical it certainly is, that since our entry into the EEC there is scarcely an address in Britain that isn't shouting for home, sweet home rule.

That's all.

No, it still isn't.

What sort of world is it in which you can live in Earl's Court all your life and still get cards pushed through your letter-box, offering you English lessons? *Read on.*

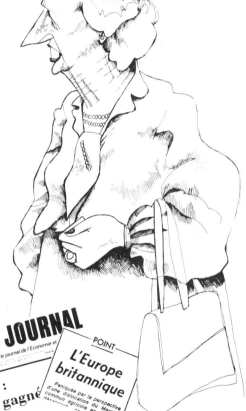

EURO-TOURISTS

(with no apologies whatsoever to John Masefield's *Cargoes*)

Charabancs from Hanover with dismal chauffeurs
Parked all over London on double-yellow lines
With a cargo of Kraut-heads
Armed with their Ach-to-Zeds
Leicas and *lederhosen,* ugly schweins!

Evil-smelling Belgians rowing across the Channel
To shop for decent underwear at Marks and Sparks
Tourist chiefs solicit us
Be nice to our visitors
Well, thank you, Hermann Goering, for our National Car Parks.

Grotty Froggy students with their sweat-stained haversacks
'Où est la rue de Carnaby? Les YMCA's?'
Piccadilly Circus
Is littered with their takeaways
One shudders every time one hears the Marseillaise.

(and no apologies whatsoever to them either)

EURO HISTORY

Prehistoric Europe

Some time after 'In the beginning was the', round about the first Wednesday afternoon in God's Calendar, or 200 million years ago or so in ours, in the Palaeozoic Age (as those who could spell knew it at the time), the continents began to extricate themselves from the Almighty's one great heap. They began to jockey for position, bumping and grinding, steaming and bubbling at about 3,000,000° Centigrade (Gas Mark 789).

Pangaea started to split. America, for instance, heaved itself off the coast of Africa; at the time, New York was nose-down in a Moroccan beach, and headed west, young man. Asia stretched and settled east, lowering its great bum into the China Sea. Australasia headed for the sand and surf. India kissed goodbye to Antarctica and made for the equator. Stirring times! Europe then made its first decision as a land-mass and shunted north, out of the warm.

It could have been worse. Had Europe not dragged its last leg and caught the big toe of Italy on a bit of Libya and fallen flat on its Iberian head, it might well not have stopped until it reached the Arctic Circle. If the shape of Europe is like nothing more than a drunken hunchback prostrate in the Mediterranean, then the British Isles are a mandrill sitting on its shoulder, clutching a green box full of nuts. As Europe lurched, the sturdy little anthropoid leapt for freedom into the seething Atlantic, hoping perhaps in a last desperate effort to make it to the West Indies or the coast of Florida. Alas, it sank 20 miles out, perched on the Continental Shelf.

So there we are. And instead of being black or tanned, warm and loose-limbed and – dare I say it – passionate, we evolved through the ever-increasing mist and rain, winds light to variable, as white and spotty, chill and tight-lipped and – dare I say it – not really very, all in all.

A brief history of Europe Repeats itself

THE ROMANS

The first attempt to unify Europe socially and politically was made by the Romans, and a pretty fair fist they made of it. For over 400 years, membership extended from the steaming cits and supermarkets of Mesopotamia on the right to Hadrian's Wall at the top left, thus drawing the line quite properly at a lot of A-rabs and Picts. Free trade was encouraged, which meant that Alexandrian purveyors of carpets, or of the latest in djellabas and hard-porn tiling, could work the High Street, Berwick-on-Tweed, while Newcastle could send coal to Thrace. Latin became the 'lingua Brusselese'.

The Romans considered Britain to be 'backward', which would seem the place to be, but they established the City of London for us and gave us the A1, the A4 and Reigate bypass.

The encouraging sign for pro-Europeans is that they did succeed in turning Europe into a suburb of Rome. The discouraging sign is what happened to the Roman Empire ultimately. Consult your Gibbon.

It bleeding declined and fell, mate

Eurofact: *The Romans, by posting several black African legions to the Wolverhampton area, produced an interesting ethnic type still lurking today.*

If this fascinating sociological fact causes people in the Wolverhampton area to look at themselves in a new light, then my living has not been in vain. Why, as I wrote that, did Felix Mendhellson and his Hawaiian Serenaders leap to mind? They kept us going through the war with their emotive renderings of Aloha, Thing and had a strip in Radio Fun. Does the fact that the last time I flew into Paris I found myself humming Tulips from Amsterdam *explain anything? Discuss.*

Further encouraging historical note – and proof positive that if you need a bit of spiritual uplift, consult the histories and you will find you are never alone – the Romans had no idea about organising industrial production. When I read that they lacked economic forethought, I felt I could withstand all that Mother Thatcher has to offer. H. A. L. Fisher writes in his *History of Europe* that 'the devaluation of the coinage during the third century brought about the ruin of the middle-class'. This, of course, is apparent to all who have stooped in Uriconium or the like and found the ground littered with handfuls of small change which seems to have been tossed about in the most cavalier manner, particularly in the bathroom. Did it fall out of the citizens' trousers as they were folding them? Doesn't history repeat itself? They were also extremely careless with crockery and footwear.

Q How do you equate the extraordinary military efficiency of the Roman soldier with his counterpart in World War II, who spent most of his time holding his woolly hat on with both hands?

A Those who inherited any talent with the short sword or catapult went into organised crime as we know it, and became hit-men for the Mafiosa or moved into the back four for Juventus.

Q If Claudius was boring and suffered a speech impediment, Caligula disgusting in his personal habits, not to mention his sisters, and Nero not only mad but a rotten violinist, what were they?

A A lot more fun than Roy Jenkins nonetheless.

THERE ARE WETS UNDER MY BED !

BOADICEA, The Iron Lady of the Iceni. Is this what those wags in Whitehall were thinking of when they called Mrs T - Attila The Hen?

WE SINK-A YOU IN-A THE PYLON UNDER THE WATLING ST FLY-OVER

COSA NOSTRA IV

Great Euro-Persons

LEO THE ISAURIAN

Now there are those who will say that the reason the cry of the muezzin is unknown in St John's Wood, that Ali Baba and the Forty Shop-Lifters are not pillaging Oxford Street, that the whirling of the dervish is unknown in Saudi-Kensington, that armies of little fat ladies in black robes and Lone Ranger masks do not totter round Sainsbury's weighed down with wire-basket-loads of pan-scourers and brown rice, that convoys of Mercedes Benz do not disgorge pampered jades of Asia into Harrods by the minute, is entirely the work of one man – namely Charles Martel the Frank, father of Pippin the Short, who up-ended the Saracen hordes at Poitiers in 732. Such people will totally ignore the weightier claims of Leo the Isaurian.

But, but, he stuttered in righteous bile, for Leo, Emperor of Byzantium and complete stranger to the xylophone, holding out in Constantinople (717, and a minute later at 7.18) the Moslem hordes would have been up the Balkans, streaming through the Urals, and double-parked in Harley Street in a jiffy. I think I speak for all of us when I say 'Bully for you, Leo the Isaurian'.

> **Q** Do you sometimes get the feeling history is being made all over you?
>
> **A** Daily.

My wives don't understand me

Books which may be consulted:
Mohammed and the Rise of Islam   D. S. Margoliouth (1905)
The Origins of Islam in its Christian Environment   R. Bell (1926)
The Benefits of Islam   Knight, Frank and Rutley
The Jubilee Book of Cricket   Prince K. S. Ranjitsinhji
Casino Real (A Farci-Tragedy in Three Acts)   Tennessee Ernie Ladbroke

THE EMPEROR CHARLEMAGNE

Charlemagne was next up to try and whip Europe into one – with new, added Christianity. He had a moustache, eight wives, fourteen children, was semi-illiterate and heavily into pagan-bashing. You'll be sorry to hear that the Saxons under Widukind were particularly hard-hit. Indeed, after Charlemagne wasted some 5,000 hostages, Widukind subjected himself hurriedly to a thorough going-over in the font.

Like many muscular Christians since, Charlemagne recognised the power of the bent knee, particularly when brought up sharply into the nether regions of your pagan. His own Frankish clergy being equally brutish and in their missionary zeal tending to give blessings straight between the eyes, subtler approaches to the soul were left to visiting Irish and English monks. You can catch up on their activities in the ecclesiastical history of the Venerable Bede, who rather wisely never ventured south of Sunderland on hearing that the Frogs knew him as 'Le Bidet Vénérable', which could have led to scenes that beggar description.

Another holy roller who deserves a round is St Boniface who, leaving his old side-kick, Willibrod, to convert Frisia, went off to sort out the Germans for 35 years. During that time he persuaded countless Hessians, Thuringians and Bavarians to trade in their jackboots for the remedial sandal. Would that he were with us today. Alas, he returned to Frisia to see how old Willibrod was doing with the Frisians, and was sharply martyred there. And the ungrateful buggers moo so contentedly today.

Charlemagne himself seen here at the kick-off of the first final of the European Cup Winners' Cup Winners' Cup. His horse scored from the centre spot. This led to a massive revision of the rules, and today only white police horses and Crazy Emlyn Hughes are allowed near the park.

Final score: Transylvania 2 (Horse 1, The Voivoide 1) Franks 3 (Pippin, a hat-trick).

Thus, by the end of his reign, Charlemagne had most of the Market as we know it under his thrall. He had also been crowned Emperor of the Holy Roman Empire by a pleased Pope – quite unexpectedly, apparently, if eye-witnesses are to be believed. He was getting up off his knees after a routine 'Bless you etc' when on went the crown and, to a man, the crowd ad-libbed loudly: *'Karolo piissimo augusto a Deo Coronato vita et victoria!!'* As you can see, Latin was back in a big way, and sliding easily off the tongue. But then all Europe was now under the Papal auspice, which could only lead to another massive revision of the rules, and fewer mounted Popes.

Everything could well have remained as one after the death of Charlemagne, but for the customary disgraceful behaviour of relatives at such a time. Many the aunt at the death-bed who has been caught going through the recently deceased's pockets, and when questioned lied feebly that she was hunting for a Kleenex.

The charmingly entitled Louis le Debonnaire took over. ('Charmingly entitled', that is, until you discover that in French it means Louis the Pious, which shows how little they know.) On his death, the carve-up started. His three sons were Charles the Bald, Lewis the German, and Lothair, who despite his name may well have been bald and indeed German and God only knows what besides, but obviously didn't think it worthy of a mention. They indulged in a vast punch-up at Fontenay, as a result of which they then agreed on a split. Europe was back to square one, where it belongs.

SOME GOOD NEWS FOR BRITS

The best public library north of the Alps in those days was in York. I only throw this in because they'll probably pull it down any moment now.

SOME BAD NEWS FOR BRITS

Offa, King of Mercia at the time, produced gold coins with 'Offa, Rex' on one side and, wait for it, *Arabic* on the back. This I toss into the bottomless well of your knowledge in order that when they announce shortly that the pound note is to be similarly sub-titled, you can say glibly 'Not for the first time, ducky!' and feel slightly brighter on an otherwise dark day.

I'M AN OFFA THEY CAN'T REFUSE

OFFA'S DYKE

Q What did Boniface get for converting a Hessian?

A Two points and a sainthood.

Q What did Willibrod get for converting a Frisian?

A Two pints please.

Q What do you get if you cross Lord Goodman with a team of Sherpas?

A A Duke of Edinburgh Award and life membership of the Royal Geographical Society.

WILLIAM WEY

Euro-tourism in the Middle Ages was confined in the main to the pilgrimage, which smacks at best of 14 days in Gatwick. What roads there were were stiff with vagabonds, pedlars, actors, men of God and crawling flagellants. Mugging, of course, was rife, and when traffic was below peak and potential muggees rare, the lads would nick the road. They could flog off large lumps of it as building materials. This caused a further hazard for the traveller – large pot-holes, of sufficient size when rain-filled to provide a watery grave for any passing horse

It's the horse I'm worried about.

and rider. The same effect today is achieved by the juggernaut, which is quickly undermining the fabric of society as we know it: viz., causing roads to give way, houses to fall down and contributing about as much to the quality of life as the neutron bomb.

As if the roads weren't bad enough, the bridges were none too chipper either. They had this laughable habit of building houses and shops on them, and while that may have made life easier for the primitive plumber, they were given (as in the case of London Bridge, probably built from the fast lane of Old Wapping High Street) to unexpected collapse. (Again – see Juggernauts.)

Juggernauts

Do you remember (and they've pulled down Memory Lane to make room for the bastards) when juggernauts used to have little discs on the back advertising their speed limit? Do you remember when they used to have indicators? How times have changed. Nowadays one of the thrills of travel is watching three of the brutes juggernaut-racing up a gradient on the M1. Brussels thinks they should be larger.

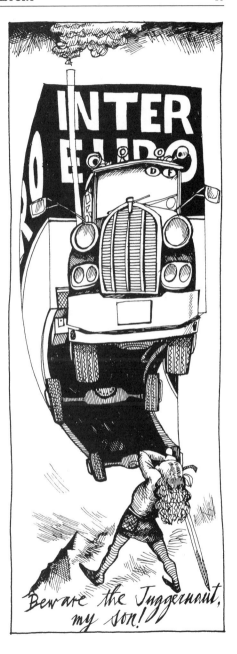

Beware the Juggernaut, my son!

Q Whence comes the word 'juggernaut'?

A I only know because I came upon it in *Dr Jekyll and Mr Hyde*. Mr Hyde is first encountered walking briskly home, and carelessly treading on an eight-year-old girl. 'It wasn't like a man', says our narrator, 'it was like some damned juggernaut'. I had to look it up. The word comes from the Hindi. One of the Krishna's nom-de-plumes is 'Jagannath', and they had this cheery custom in those parts of mounting his image in a large cart and, while it was dragged through the streets, religious nuts would hurl themselves under the wheels. Get crushed for Krishna! 'It has come to mean', says the book, 'anything which ruthlessly tramples or mows down what lies in its way'. Oh, happy happenstance!

Meanwhile, back in the Middle Ages.

Back in the Middle Ages, as today, motorway facilities were pretty rugged, road-houses and comfort-stations being at a premium. In the early fourteenth century, for an outlay of about two shillings and threepence in old, proper money (which is roughly our eleven new pence and no better for that and, given inflation, about £93) you could get bread, meat, a firkin of ale, horse-fodder, a candle and a good bundle of rat-infested straw and a flea-packed blanket which you put in a box and slept with. Quite often you were obliged to make room in your box for a fellow-traveller.

There was invariably some form of in-house entertainment. A miller, perhaps, with a rattling good yarn about sticking his arse ('a handsome piece of work' as I recall) out of a window and breaking wind violently into the face of a rival as he puckered up to kiss what he presumed to be his paramour. Or at cabaret time, there might be a roving troubadour with a ballad or two about the horrors of modern living, and fickleness of housewives. *Plus ça change*, eh? Only the prices have been changed to line the pocket of the guilty. On your horse, pilgrim.

Enter left William Wey

Really to impress the neighbours, the thing to be was a palmer. The rude equivalent of wintering in Mustique, it meant you'd done the Holy Land. Instead of showing off your suntan or slides, you asked people round to study your palm-fronds. There were regular excursions from Venice and this is where William Wey comes in, the father of the tourist guide. He was not the first to venture into this area, but the least fanciful to date and far less alarmist. Previous works had warned the tourist against unicorns, dragons, oliphants, ogres, werewolves and short men with faces peering out of their stomachs. They recommended trips to fountains of youth and the like: William Wey was more practical. For instance, given the shoddy cut-price practices of the average Venetian tour operative, he points his readers to a Milletts behind St Mark's Cathedral where you could pick up bed and bedding for three ducats, with half your money back on the empty, regardless of wear and tear.

He warns, quite rightly, against the perils of foreign food and drink, singing the praises of a good bowel-binder, available at most apothecaries. His book lists simple phrases like 'How much?', gives the current exchange rates, and a number of sightseeing trips in the Holy Land. The unwary traveller is constantly alerted against confidence-tricksters, particularly suave Saracens. The tourist is also reminded that there is a bandit behind every palm tree.

Eurofact: *In 1188 the average time taken for a letter to travel from Rome to Canterbury by fast horse was 29 days. The average monk would cover the same ground in 49 days. Aggrieved remark overheard in Rome from one who had missed the last fast horse: 'There's never an average monk when you want one.'*

THE THIRD CRUSADE

Famous Knight sets out on Third Crusade.

It's all been done before, and rarely more so than in the Third Crusade.

Richard the Lionheart was in many ways a right bastard. His first act on his accession was to flog off everything he could in the public sector. Bishoprics, baronetcies, castles, some two or three times over, all were on offer.*

(It makes one wonder idly whether Mrs Thatcher's own efforts in that direction are motivated by an urge to conquer inflation, or in fact to invade Poland.)

Adequately financed, Richard went to France to meet Philip Augustus and they headed south, arguing ceaselessly – mainly about Richard's sudden decision not to marry the French king's sister. Philip accused him of breach of promise and agreed to settle out of court for an annual 2,000 marks. 'Such', says dear old Hume, 'were the heroes of this pious enterprise'.

The Crusade itself was a wonderful Euro-enterprise. The French, with their catapult aptly named The Bad Neighbour, left for an early bath, Richard massacred 2,600 Saracen hostages on a point of order, and the Franks were constantly devious. Conrad of Montfenat was assassinated and Richard blamed. The weather was appalling, they were forced to eat horse (see French Cuisine) and Richard made an enemy for life of Duke Leopold of Austria (a) by taking his banner down after the two of them had taken Acre and replacing it with his own, and (b) kicking him in the trousers when the Duke refused to help rebuild the walls at Ascalon. Having failed to win the cup, Richard signed a three-year treaty with Saladin, which upset everybody, and decided to go home – rather foolishly, by walking through Austria. Not unnaturally, the Duke hijacked him, causing further Euro-furore. 'We ought to do this more often', sang Blondin the Troubadour, a fine light tenor but pig-ignorant.

*At one stage he appeared eager to put London itself on the market, but Arabs in those days being strictly battle-axe-fodder, there were no takers. The reason for this hyper-auction was to get him into Palestine, where the action was, and where glory lay. Jerusalem, the World Cup of its day, was presently held by Saladin.

En passant

I remember thinking it odd when I was in the Army in Germany in 1956, holding back the Russian hordes, that the German police were better armed than I was. This may be in breach of the Official Secrets Act, but what the hell, as far as I am aware the only weapon with which I was equipped to resist the Red Army was a typewriter. Throw the typewriter at Boris and run like hell for Ostend was one plan I'd formulated, and no one, from the C-in-C downwards, had given me a better. Plan two came to me on noticing that the local plods had large truncheons and small pistols. Plan two: throw the typewriter at Boris, mug a constable, and bash and shoot my way to Ostend.

The Rewriting of European History

A captain: Here stand we now at Prince's Gate, my liege.
Sir William de Wetlaw: Yes. Sorry. Prompt?
Prompt Corner: The British people . . .
Sir William de Wetlaw: Yes?
Prompt Corner: The British people will not tolerate this sort of thing.
Sir William de Wetlaw: Ah, yes.

(All's Well That Ends Will   Act V)

Q What is all that about, you bushy-faced elk?

A Many have wondered why, after the successful SAS onslaught on the Iranian Embassy, William Whitelaw, the home secretary, was at the press conference, wild-eyed and breathless, close to hysteria, some said, while others feared a fit. The truth is that he was first in, balaclava-helmeted and armed to the gunwales, having been lowered on several ropes and pushed through an upper window. (He was followed in by Archbishop Runcie, similarly attired.) The rest is history. Remember that you read it here first.

There was no such drama in Richard's case. After some time in durance vile, he was arraigned before the Diet of Worms, and got off with a ransom of about 300 grand.

A grinding halt

Q Why have you stopped, bearded weirdo?

A I have just read two things that have caused me to pause in my breathtaking dash through European history, undertaken, as you will doubtless have gathered, to prove that

(1) we have never liked them and, to be fair, you can't blame them, that they are none too fond of us and
(2) our attempts to be as one have been as fruitless as John Ruskin's marriage-bed.

I read that the EEC is currently engaged in financing a research project to find a more truly European attitude to history, which reeks a little of a formal Russian education – Lenin invented the bicycle chain, Molotov the hovercraft etc.

Then I read something Bernard Levin (a name to injure with) wrote in 1975 on the eve of the referendum. To use this, is, I confess, a little unfair, and not dissimilar to reading what the Derby tipsters mooted after the race is run. However . . . 'I shall vote Yes tomorrow', he wrote, 'because I believe that the EEC has proved the best staging-post on the road away from what the late Desmond Donnelly, in an inspired phrase, called "the European Civil War that spanned the years from 1914 to 1945"'! A touch glib in my view. A little facile, Bernard.

I suppose World War I could be written off given the Kaiser and Edward VII and the Tsar as an inter-Euro-family scuffle (see Charles the Bald, Lothair etc), and 50 per cent of World War II can be laid firmly at the feet of the beastly Japanese. I've seen it argued that Adolf Hitler had no idea World War II was in progress. It could, I suppose, be further argued that in the wider sense, a United Europe was his brainchild.

The names on the local war memorial can be explained as unsolved murders and traffic accidents in the area. But . . .

Meanwhile in Brussels

I think Henry V was next on my list of Great Europeans. I was going to indulge in a little patriotic judder with myself. It is to be hoped that you would have joined me outside Harfleur, 'Once more unto the breach . . . greyhounds in the slips . . . cry God for Harry, England and St George!', and come with me on a sentimental stroll through the French countryside in the steps of Hal and his clapped-out little army to Agincourt. (Now called Azincourt by the French in a crude attempt to hide the evidence.) It is current EEC thinking that European children must no longer think in terms of 'them' and 'us'. 'Think European!' must be etched into every small brain, rather as 'the wogs begin at

Calais' was to be found, after her demise, engraved on the heart of Mary Tudor.

This could lead to a deal of horse-trading (see French Cuisine again) in the Euro-classroom.

'Right', say the British commissioners (Directorate-General XII, Research, Science and Education, Directorate E, Euro-History Revision and Research, Rue de la Loi, 200, 1049 Bruxelles, if you must know) 'we shall compromise'. (Disillusioned historians and teachers, have you contemplated a career in the Euro-bureaucracy? Fat wage and bags of perks.)

'What we are offering', they continue, through the usual barrage of interpreters, 'is that, in return for your acceptance of Joan of Arc's unfortunate demise as a tragic domestic mishap involving hot fat and a primitive oven of French manufacture, we are prepared to admit that we cheated at Agincourt'.

We did, of course, in French eyes. When, in the initial charge, the flower of French chivalry was knocked off its dray-horse, the English infantrymen, as was the custom in those days, ran forward and sat on the recumbent knights's chests, thus rendering them totally useless for the remainder of the fracas and also establishing rights to a fat ransom anon for the squatting squaddie. Henry, seeing that his already depleted ranks were now being whittled almost to nil, the larger part of his army now reclining on armour-plated Froggies, he ordered all those thus seated to slit the throats of their hostages and get back into the fray. This

was extremely unpopular with the lads, but did boost our ranks and lead to two well-deserved away points. Nevertheless, it seems fair to admit these facts in exchange for Joan.

'Will you also admit', the French commissioners enquire however, 'that your victory at Poitiers was null and void, as we weren't ready?'

The British think about this for a fortnight. The difficulty of dealing with the French in this particular area – warfare – is that, despite their native keenness for things martial, the sad fact is that in the 900 years since 1066, they've never won anything. They've come a close second on a number of occasions, been well ahead at half-time, but never actually won. There is a constant fear that they could come second in a nuclear test.

On their return, the British try again. 'Right, Joan of Arc for cheating at Agincourt and Poitiers, *plus,* if you agree that Napoleon was mad, you can have the Hundred Years War.'

'Napoleon', say the French, 'was simply over-zealous in spreading his views on local government'.

'What about Waterloo?' ask the British, lighting their pipes and looking smug. Nice one, Arthur.

'A draw', say the French in French.

'Blücher won it', shout the German commissioners in German.

'Wellington!' the British cry in British.

'Was *Irish!*' cheer the Irish, leaving the interpreters for dead, and scoring *'dix points'* on the Euro-scoreboard.

Night has now fallen. It is dark outside. Brussels closes at eight. The Belgians say the last real gaiety they knew here was the Duchess of Richmond's ball. The British suddenly discover that they have agreed to give Monty's statue a beard, a palette, and a loaf of French bread, and to rename it 'Henri Rousseau', in exchange for losing Nelson's Column.

The project will finally fall into the hands of the professional myth-exploders – the Hitler-was-never-told gentlemen, and the author of 'Whodunkirk?' 'I see no little ships', says he, clapping his blind eye to the main chance.

Watch out for 'The European Civil War 1914-1945 – the Great Propaganda Exercise'. Best we forget. Best we forget.

Before the Crowned Heads of Europe, and After

Andy Warhol, one of my favourite reads, frequently asks himself – and indeed I asked myself a page or two ago, but it apparently occupies his mind whenever he's in Europe – why there were so many wars over here if the kings and queens are intermarried, because that means everybody was related, and why should people want to fight their relatives?

'Because', replies his anonymous friend, 'nobody can fight more than relatives once they get started'. Spot on the knob, baby, and we must accept some of the responsibility. For some years British diplomacy was based on (a) marrying off a royal, or (b), if that failed, sending a gunboat. This is why the royal family to this day carry spares. It could be argued that World War I would never have occurred if Victoria and Albert had practised a little self-control or even indulged in some elementary family planning.

Q What has this got to do with Europe?

A More than you think. Take King Canute, or Cnut, the rude anagram, grandson of Harold Bluetooth.

Q Why, for God's sake?

A Because we are all swept along on the tide of history, Canute or Cnut almost literally as you may recall. Nowadays, of course, the tide is out.

IN-BREEDING TELLS

In the heady days of Danegold, prior to the Norman Conquest, England was ruled by super-wet Ethelred the Extremely Unready. Such rowdy Danish elements as Swein Forkbeard and Thorkill the Tall jostled for power. Ethelred, finding it altogether too much for him, retired to Normandy. His only previous answer to the Danish problem had been to call for national fasts, of water and raw herbs. (*Plus ça change,* eh?) His one show of readiness had been to marry Emma, the Duke of Normandy's daughter, an early example of what I'm on about, but the plot further thickens. On Ethelred's death, Canute, son of Forkbeard, took over England. In a wonderful act of cynicism, Canute then married Ethelred's widow, Emma, to scotch any claims by the deceased's descendants. It didn't, and when he died they tried to cremate him, but he was too wet to burn. The whole system collapsed and led to 1066. The precedent, however, was established. Families again! (See Cain v Abel, Kramer v Kramer etc.)

Ha! you will cry, you are a republican ratbag of the worst sort. Not so, I riposte, I am a staunch royalist. Ask yourselves this simple question – if there were not a royal family, who would you put on the stamps? Who would you have on the back of your 50 pence piece? Brood carefully on that, while I gently pinpoint the unsatisfactory nature of presidents. These are invariably second-raters, failed politicians who have packed it in, or deputy prime ministers who have realised they'll never make it. I am, of course, referring to figureheads, as in Germany and Ireland and Italy, and not working presidents as in the US of A and France, though heaven knows I'm prepared to talk about it.

You have now had time to think of a British president, and have probably come up with

Harold Lever or Lord Thorneycroft. Perhaps Lord Home, he's vacant. Such speculation makes a good party game. But, ask yourselves, could you lick the back of any of them? Jangle them contentedly in your purse? Be fair.

Hence I am a royalist, and that at least should spell OBE. (No way. I was once invited for drinks at the Palace and forgot to go.) I am ever-conscious, though, that your royals are like us, essentially humanoid. Prick them and they bellow. Once, while filming down in the sewers, I was proudly shown by a Westminster Council sewage operative the actual channel that led directly from the Palace. He wept as he pointed down the arched brick tunnel. Automatically my gumboot heels crashed together, splashing his packed lunch. I admit that until that moment I'd never dwelt on that aspect of royalty. Very well, so they're not exactly like us – we haven't the facilities or the ladies of the bedchamber, etc – but we can go to the pub when we like.

En passant – as they have it in France, unlike a royal family, which they haven't, having removed it in a big way in the 1790s and I think regretted it ever since, there is after all still a finger or two of Bourbon left if they relent – en passant, a myth must be laid. The popular myth is that it is wrong to speak disparagingly or critically of our royals as they cannot defend themselves. Apart from Prince Philip, who can put the boot in with the best of them, her supporters are legion, and violent. As Malcolm Muggeridge discovered, when he once wrote a critique of the royals in *Esquire,* he unleashed upon himself such abuse, including parcels of human excrement with Cheltenham postmarks, that I fancy it led almost directly to his conversion on the road to Leatherhead. Ask Willie Hamilton if he gets off scot-free. The Yeomen of the Guard are not Her Majesty's sole buttress against the sacred cow-poke.

They could, you say, be more human, more accessible, if they were allowed to be. But do you really want a Scandinavian-style monarchy? The Queen trooping the colour mounted on a bicycle? (Incidentally, is the fact that Prince Philip isn't king contrary to the Sex Discrimination Act?)

Deepest down, I confess, I was an Edward VIII man. Born in the year of what would have

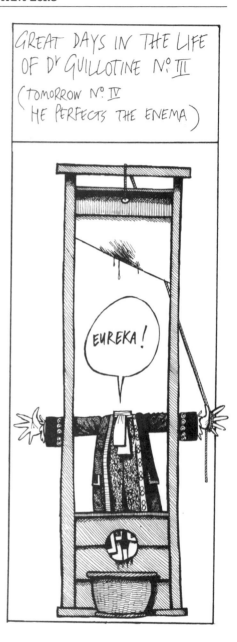

GREAT DAYS IN THE LIFE OF Dr GUILLOTINE No III
(TOMORROW No IV
HE PERFECTS THE ENEMA)

EUREKA!

been his coronation, I still have a souvenir ashtray of his. I used to have a mug as well, but the handle came off. Such was the ill-luck that dogged him through life – perhaps when young he shot an albatross. I remember thinking, as I stood in the rain on Coronation Day, 1952, in Park Lane, peering blindly through a wet periscope at a forest of wet periscopes, that it was a bit of a shame. The Queen had only got through on a bye. Poor old Edward was simply ahead of his time. What an asset an American queen would have been over the years. (Prince Charles, please note, and try to steer clear of minor European royalty and receptionists.)

Yet, there it is, the royal family; given its evolution over the years, it is probably the most European thing about us, which brings me to an interesting point.

Why, given that five members of the Nine (ourselves, Denmark, the Netherlands, Belgium and to some extent Luxembourg) have royals and only four (the Frogs, the Krauts, the Wops and the Micks) have presidents, does Europe have a president? And a Mister at that?

There's democracy in action.

President Jenkins, or next, it seems, President Thorn, smacks to my eye of banana republicanism. Not that I'd blame Her Majesty for wishing to be no part of Brussels, but whatever happened to the rest of us?

THE BIRTH OF A NOTION

A fat Penguin told me that 'the achievement of a lasting peace has been the chief motivating factor behind the drive for unity': the theory being, presumably, that the safest place to be in any future conflict will be as near to the opposition as possible. Those wrestling hand-to-hand with the enemy front line are least likely to be hit by hydrogen bombs, neutron bombs, atomic bombs, or cruise missiles, or whatever they come up with next. What the wise bird probably meant was that a United States of Europe might delay the Euro-Civil War Part 3: a peace-torn Europe being preferable to a war-torn Europe.

This must have seemed a sensible prospect in 1945 when everyone was saying 'never again' again, as they'd said in 1919. Winston Churchill has a lot to answer for, in fact, having first conceived the idea of an Anglo-French union immediately prior to France's collapse.

'The two governments declare that France and Great Britain shall no longer be two nations, but one Franco-British Union.

'Every citizen of France will enjoy immediately citizenship of Great Britain, every British subject will become a citizen of France.'

A single war cabinet, governing 'from wherever best it can. The two parliaments will be formally associated.'*

The declaration was sent to the French government in Bordeaux, and seized upon happily by Reynaud, the PM. He read it twice to his Cabinet, and 'rarely has so generous a proposal encountered such a hostile reception'. Pétain and the 'defeatists' put the kibosh on the business and I never did become Anglo-French. For, in all fairness, I must admit that after a bottle or two of something French in a Paris bistro, I can feel quite European. Rarely before midnight, though.

---

*They even produced a stamp, oblong, with our dear king's head on one side and, on the other, one of those French presidents they used to breed, with a beard you could drive through a vampire's heart.

THOUGHTS ON THE DEMISE OF CHARLES de GAULLE

The Charles de Gaulle I knew was a short, randy, red-bearded man with hairy gums and a do-it-yourself wooden leg – he'd been a cook-sergeant in the Corps Alpines, and I remember him saying that anyone who tried to whip up a lively *bouillabaisse* on skis, 15,000 feet up, deserved a wooden leg. If you think he was not as other men, you should meet the Winston Churchill I knew. He approached me once in Harrods. 'I'm Winston Churchill', he said.

'I'm Tutankhamen' I riposted, never slow with bluff repartee.

Only he really was.

And he's Tory MP for somewhere, and a bit of a lad, and all I gathered was a load of American lady tourists, eager to see my tomb.

But it was interesting to read dear old Harold's opinion of the other Charles de Gaulle, the one I didn't know, but always admired for his ability to keep us out of the Marché Commun. Isn't that interesting, by the way: I see I wrote 'dear old Harold' without a moment's thought, but nowadays we have two dear old Harolds to get sentimental about over the 8⇌11d halves of bitter: three, if you include the one with an eyeful of terminal Norman arrow. It's not a lucky name if you enter public service. No, this was dear, very old Harold Macmillan, who wrote in his diary, quoted in *The Times,* of the time he went to meet the other De Gaulle.

'I spoke', he wrote, 'very strongly to him about the free trade area and the fatal political results which would follow the present French attitude. But he clearly was neither interested nor impressed. I decided to leave a . . . letter behind and told him I would do so . . . De Gaulle, like so many soldiers of his type and period, cares nothing for "logistics".'

The first person to send in, on a coast-guard please, the three-letter word employed by the old wizard and properly excised by *The Times,* will receive by return of post, or New Year's Eve, 1984, whichever be the sooner, something French.

INS AND OUTS

At this stage in my bumbling dash through history, it all became too much for me. How has A. J. P. Taylor managed all these years? Explain the longevity of Sir Arthur Bryant. It isn't only the sharp pain between the eyeballs as one is forced to face facts again, it's the dull ache at the back of the brain caused by opening and slamming shut long-emptied filing cabinets. Proof positive in my case that 'A'-levels don't last. Old men forget.

Anyway, my brain snapped, Captain Oates staggered from the tent, and there's never a taxi when you want one. When one looks back at those sad days when we gave it all away to enter Europe, the tears begin to well. I really don't know how historians get through the day. What we all need from our politicos is a little wisdom *before* the event. Albeitmoresoever, let us all go down the dismal, damp, cobbled stone passages of British entry into Europe, where the sun that never set on the British Empire so rarely rises.

INSPIRED BY E.C.S.C. AND DESPITE FROG FEAR OF BOCHE RE-ARMAMENT, EURO-DEFENCE THING FORMED 1952. U.K. STAY OUT.

1953. A EURO-POLITICAL THING IS MOOTED. FRANCE, FEARING SUPRA-NATIONALISM, KILL IT OFF. U.K. AVOID IT LIKE PLAGUE.

1955. THE SIX, PLUS U.K., BEGIN DISCUSSING CREATION OF E.E.C. FRANCE NOT KEEN. U.K. WALK OUT.

1957

THE TREATY OF ROME IS SIGNED.

BOSH!

AM BEEGER ZAN ZIS SING

'ALLO

RIGHT— WE'VE STILL GOT THE EMPIRE — WE'LL SPLIT EUROPE IN HALF BY FORMING EFTA — AND - ER — THEN WE'LL APPLY TO JOIN THE COMMON MARKET —

Good thinking, sir!

LET ZE GÜT TIMES ROLL

TRÈS SEXY

WUNDERBAR!

Bonne Chance

Le Six

A Night to Remember

I invariably lie about my activities on the night we officially entered Europe. I've put it about since that I held out in the snug bar of *The Legless Newsreader* until three in the morning after the night before, refusing to be budged, and shouting: *'Maintenant je suis européen, et nous n'avons pas de licensing laws. Piss off! Allez-vous-en! Raus machen!'* and, as it's my only word of Italian, *'Prego! Prego!'* which sounds right and quite polite the way I put it.

In fact, of course, the abolition of those daft laws, only created during World War I to protect munitions-workers from themselves, would have given us all cause to believe that there were some benefits to be accrued from entry. Suddenly driving on the wrong side of the road would have added a little excitement and zest to the occasion as well, but none of this was to be. In truth, I was in position to make Rushton's Last Stand, as I was on the fourth floor of BBC Television Centre, next to Weather, recording an instalment of *Up Sunday*. This was an extremely late-night programme on the BBC, which a few of you may remember with affection and thus risk beatification; or the name may mean nothing at all, which places you firmly in the same intellectual bracket as the Tory minister of education who thinks charisma is 25 December.

The programme started just before 11 o'clock, which, we realised, was midnight as far as Europe was concerned – it not yet being blessed with the vagaries of British summertime (and the living ain't easy). Thus, in Euro-terms, we were already in. Any church-bells, fireworks, whistles, maroons or whoopee-cushions that HM Government had prepared for midnight our time would have been an hour late, and totally irrelevant.

After some years, which in Brussels terms is as swift as salts through a short Indian, a European Summertime Policy (ESP) has been adopted. This means that Euro-summer will now begin on 29 March in 1981, and in 1982 on 28 March. This is something of a triumph of

compromise, as the British are now delaying their usual opening day for a week, while Europe is preparing to embark on the season a week earlier. Now, in your innocence, you might suppose that, while your pen is poised over the diary, they might seize the opportunity to provide you with appropriate closing dates, too. Not so. The British will still be straw-hatted and white-flannelled until 26 October, while your continental will have packed away his Ambre Solaire and rubber duck by 28 September.

Meanwhile, back on *Up Sunday* on that stirring eve, we celebrated with a tasteless little sketch in which I appeared in Edward Heath's bed as a saucy French matelot, a gift from Monsieur Pompidou. Why, I have no idea, but it seemed splendidly satirical at the time. You can never be certain what might bring a government to its knees, and suffice to say that the lisping Gallic gaiety of my performance led to my one and only appearance in a Euro-movie. In it I played Tim Brooke-Taylor's husband, though happily this was not a physical role, and I was fully tweeded throughout. I had a telling, dramatic scene in an antique shop in the Camden Passage, in which I was obliged to break down when he upped and left me and finally die of shock when Sharon Tate, clad only in a mackintosh, bent over my prostrate form, revealing to the shattered old pooftah the mysteries of the female chest. (True acting is to register in a single look that I much preferred Brooke-Taylor's.)

Some of the problems of the new Europe were revealed to me as well: language, for instance. The director was French, the crew Anglo-Franco-Italian and the leading man, Vittoria Gassman, Italian. As a result, the film was shot without sound, each actor working in his native tongue, while, in the language of signs and Babel, the director, cameraman etc carried on communicating throughout the action. To make it simpler for the dubbing later, the speaker was invariably shot from behind, in the Sicilian manner, or made to put his hands over his mouth. What a fine time to be bearded. The thing I enjoyed most about spaghetti westerns was the animated bands of Italian Apaches, all gesticulating away over the wampum; I did a distinguished cameo at Cinecitta outside Rome, the scene being John o'Groats in heavy winter, and the Italian extras in kilts and woolly hats were almost as good.

The other Euro-for-instance was quite beastly. Six weeks after the movie was concluded, Sharon Tate, who was a most delightful and beautiful creature, was murdered in Los Angeles in the most grotesque circumstances. At once, the cast was rushed into sound studios all over Europe to add the necessary words. The greed and speed of it all was appalling, but I don't think the film ever saw the light of night. I never knew what it was called. I couldn't translate the title.

Stunning facts you should know from the EEC Statistical Services's latest hit *Social Indicators for the European Community.*

Q How long does a Belgian have to work to earn a kilo of cod fillets, not bread-crumbed, in carton?

A 59 minutes. It takes a Froggy 1 hour 49 minutes.

Q Where is a woman most likely to be killed in a traffic accident?

A Belgium. France concentrates hardest on male deaths.

Q Which country has the most out-houses?

A Belgium again.

Q Where is cirrhosis of the liver most rife?

A France, where, of course, they drink like fish.

Q Where will I find teenage fertility at its zenith?

A Italy.

Q Where is the highest employment level?

A Denmark, but a word to the wise, they also lead in divorce and suicide.

Q Where will I live longest?

A The Netherlands. The men live for 71.5 years and the women for 78, but I can't recommend it.

Q Which country do most people leave each year?

A Luxembourg. Isn't this exciting?

Q Where do they go?

A I've no idea. I've never met one.

Q Who stay longest in hospital?

A The British, hooray! Is it surprising?

The Great Referendum

I would define a debate, if asked, as something at which one sits and listens with an open mind to opposing views thoughtfully put, then mulls over the arguments that are subsequently bandied about, makes up one's aforementioned open mind, and finally rises and strides manfully through the 'Ayes' or 'Nos'.

Admittedly, this can lead you to sit out the occasional *danse macabre* as a don't-know. I remember Richard Dimbleby, God's own umpire, adjudicating between two economists as they discussed the advantages of revaluation over devaluation, and vice versa, and finding at the end of it that I agreed wholeheartedly with both of them.

Listening and mulling seem to have gone out of the window nowadays. I have never pointed the finger at a politician who changed his mind. When probing media-men shout excitedly 'Ah, but minister, in 1958 you said . . . '. This is simply an exercise in nostalgia, and invariably means that some research assistant has traipsed down memory lane and pressed a few doorbells.

Thus when Harold Wilson (a man for the grand entrance as long as he knew where the exit was) made his famous comeback in February 1974, I was prepared to allow him a fresh start. His first act was to announce the great renegotiation once he'd routed Heath from Number 10. (Heath, his great fingers still wrapped tightly around a leg of the Bechstein Grand, had been reluctantly ousted, and the great juddering body was sent round in a pantechnicon to Norman St John Stevas, who, demonstrating that deeply sensitive nature we have come slowly to mistrust totally, read *Sea Fever* for a week to the weeping Heath.)

Labour had said that they were in favour of Common Market entry if the terms were right and Heath and Co, in their over-eagerness and unnatural excitement, had misunderstood them. Thus Honest Jim Callaghan of the Foreign Office – bluff, hale and devious – was immediately sent in. Initially, with heavy boots on. Tough talk of *fundamental*

renegotiations caused a few hearts of oak to flutter. Did this mean that the Treaty of Rome would be taken apart page by page, perhaps? That there would be no admission for foreigners? That the Six would join the Commonwealth (well, Five of them anyway: Luxembourg would be part of Kent)? That there would be free drinks on the French? Not quite, alas, but Jim was in ugly mood. You could tell this by his amiable look and explosive Eeyore of a laugh. (A further word of advice: if you ever see Sir Keith Joseph smile – emigrate!)

Any trouble, Jim intimated to the Council of Ministers, while gritting his lips and adjusting the length of rubber hose in his trousers as he spoke, and we'll be off. It was 1 April, but perhaps the continentals don't celebrate the date in the same way as we do. I can't imagine they would convene a Council of Ministers on All Fools' Day if they did. They are darkly superstitious folk, and have taken once more to hanging garlic round their beds whenever Mrs Thatcher crosses the Channel.

By June, Jim was all sweetness and light and, apart from one bizarre moment when Dr Fitzgerald, the Irish Minister, announced that Mr Callaghan's figures were 'arithmetically impossible' and held up 12 fingers to prove it, the other Eight seemed relatively sympathetic to the new non-violent approach. Most acceptable to them was Callaghan's assurance that no re-write of the Treaty of Rome was necessary. As any activity in that direction would cause brain damage and double hernias, one can understand their low whistles of relief. Basically, Labour's idea was that Britain should be a member, but should not pay through the nose for this privilege. I preferred his April Fool approach.

Albeitmoresoever, agreement was reached in March 1975, Wilson and Callaghan pronounced themselves content, and the Great Referendum was on. Of course, the only way it could be exciting was if the 'Nos' leapt into an early lead and, indeed, stayed there. I've never been able, I'm afraid, to think of the European movement as a forward one. Europe has become one of those places one sets out *from,* rather than gets *into.* A 'Yes' vote could be compared with the Pilgrim Fathers setting out from Plymouth and alighting excitedly at Folkestone, or the great American wagon trains going east. The pioneering spiritual uplift we all need so desperately in these grey days requires wide, open spaces, fresh fields and pastures new. It's all very well to point out Chartres Cathedral as an example of the sort of thing we Europeans do so well, but I think one is entitled to ask 'What have you done since, Chartres?'

The Government have announced the results of the renegotiation of the United Kingdom's terms of membership of the European Community.

DO YOU THINK THAT THE UNITED KINGDOM SHOULD STAY IN THE EUROPEAN COMMUNITY (THE COMMON MARKET)?

YES ☐

NO ☐

Briefly, the opposing arguments, precursors of the waffle mountain, were as follows:

YES	NO
Europe is a Great Thing, an ideal, a great vision, a Great Thing.	
	Rubbish. It is a continental dog's breakfast.
We must rise above lesser issues and worries. Europe spells peace and prosperity.	No, it doesn't.
We cannot go it alone.	We shan't be alone.

YES	NO
Europe is exciting and challenging.	No, it isn't.
It will increase our influence in world affairs.	Not at all.
Can you think of any prospect more enticing than economic and monetary union?	Yes. Participating in a round-the-world three-legged race partnered by Lord Chalfont.

YES	NO
One day we shall all have nice, mauve Euro-passports.	Yuck.
We've got to get in to get on!	Get out!
Think of the future. Think of your children.	We are.
Europe can provide a sense of vocation. *(Soames)*	What?
Only by serving a vision of something better and more noble than ourselves can we achieve that poise and sense of balance and dignity that have so often been the envy of the world. *(Soames again)*	Speak for yourself, fatty.
The EEC offers excellent opportunities for those with artistic gifts and skills who are willing to use them with enterprise and energy. *(Lord Elwyn-Jones, then Lord Chancellor)*	Hollow laughter: ho! ho! ho! *(Rushton)*

Bernard Levin

Why leave the lifeboat for a sea full of sharks?

They're a jollier type of person.

YES	NO
What are the alternatives?	Herewith a parable related by Denis Healey (whom God preserve). During the Lisbon earthquake a travelling salesman was discovered roaming the streets shouting loudly: 'Pills against the earthquake! Pills against the earthquake!' When some pedant pointed out that pills were no proof against earthquakes, the pusher replied sagely: 'What are the alternatives?'

There were of course further arguments such as the Wilsonian 'A "Yes" vote is a vote for more jobs', the advantage of Common Market membership to the steel industry and agriculture, the fact that we needed a period of peace and stability, which in the foulness of time seem to fall a little short of sound.

Tick makes Home Office cross

An advertisement by the National Referendum Campaign showing a tick instead of a cross in the " No " box on a referendum ballot paper might cause a lot of confusion, the Home Office said yesterday.

Later, Mr Ronald Leighton, the campaign's press officer, said: " I take the point. It would be better to show a cross."

Excitement too much for some.

The Great Debate

One positive result of the Common Market is the creation of strange bed-fellows and, whereas in the normal run of events one would naturally prefer to find oneself in bed with Shirley Williams rather than Peter Shore, there are moments when such considerations must be set aside. It has to be admitted, however, that even the most hardened sexologist would baulk at some of the couplings.

Here is an example. As the poet sang, 'Who does what? And with which? And to whom?'

What a ruckus, what a rumpus there should have been. Hopes were high that we'd be swept along on tides of oratory, yodelling with delight, while boring old party politics were forgotten. We'd expected brother to oppose brother, brothers, and Tories to reach for their battle-axes, tell them tenderly they'd be late home from the office, and go to work on each other. Instead, there was all the excitement of Sir Geoffrey Howe reading the meter to the hard of hearing. Most of the speeches would have been more happily delivered by Pickfords.

ITV TONIGHT 9.10

GRANADA TELEVISION

Look Both Ways before you Vote

A debate in Parliamentary form

MOTION:

'That Britain should remain in the European Economic Community'

PROPOSED BY

Edward Heath

OPPOSED BY

Enoch Powell

Winding up AGAINST

Tony Benn

Winding up FOR

Roy Jenkins

Chairman: Rt. Hon. Betty Harvie Anderson, MP (former Deputy Speaker)

The Great Debaters

Two persons who managed to keep their heads above porridge-level throughout the Great Debate were Enoch Powell and Peter Shore.

Enoch Powell had a field day. Those of us with our buckets full tend to dissociate themselves speedily from his views on immigration, but when the mild, bulging eyes are narrowed and their piercing gaze is directed at the Market, it's like watching Vivian Richards at the wicket. Watch the old white hunter spread a luxuriant Persian rug over the worm-packed floorboards in the Conservative lobby, and sit back listening for the squawks as his prey fall into the cellars.

'I cannot but believe', he said, 'that Conservatives in the bulk are bound to revert to the natural stance of a Conservative, which is defence of our national independence and of our parliamentary institutions'. Squawk. Thud. Squawk. Thud. Squawk. Thud. At least.

He praised effusively Mrs Thatcher's technique of keeping her head below the parapet. 'I think the lady is very wise. If there is no long-term remaining in the EEC for Britain, there is no point in the new Conservative leadership spiking itself irrevocably on the commitments of the former discredited Conservative leadership.' More thumps. More squawks. He's talking daggers.

Jolly insights into the animosity between himself and E. Heath were revealed: 'I would dearly have liked to be friends. But like everyone else, I found it impossible.' And, when asked if he would stand by the results of the referendum, he replied that he could see no reason why the referendum result should be regarded as final. Was non-irrevocability, he asked innocently, not the essence of sovereignty and parliamentary democracy? Exit right the smiler with the knife.

As for Peter Shore, it's interesting to look at two debates in which he took part at the Oxford Union. One took place a few days prior to the referendum, and the other was held in June 1980. The first motion in June 1975 was 'That this house would say "Yes" to Europe'. P. Shore and Barbara Castle were ranged against Jeremy Thorpe and Edward Heath – rather more likely bed-fellows (than in the Granada television programme, that is). The most enlivening question raised was what the likes of P. Shore and B. Castle, violently anti-Market Cabinet members, would do after the referendum. Thorpe suggested they might perhaps hang about on full pay, like five maggots in the European apple.

'If the vote is "Yes",' replied Mrs Castle spiritedly, 'my country will need me'.

Mr Shore said that it was high time the populace at large was asked for their opinion

Hats Off to the Don't-Knows
The only ones to emerge from the grisly business with credit were the 'don't-know' campaigners. They conducted a survey which revealed that 51 per cent of those questioned did not know the meaning of EEC. They also forecast that 35 per cent of the electorate did not plan to vote which, in the event, was smack on the button. Could this be the political party we're all seeking? They seem to have a substantial power-base.

on the EEC. Mr Heath had never asked a soul.

'I hope you will appreciate', he hoped, 'that in the Treaty of Rome, Britain now has its first constitution, one to which no Briton has contributed. The power of deciding the laws of our country is the centre of democracy.'

Mr Heath (the former president of the Union) then rose and announced for no very good reason that he had 'denounced the Munich agreement from this very box'. (This was greeted with cries of 'So what, sailor?' and tittering.) 'The main difference between the two sides is not over prices, jobs or tariffs but', he continued, shifting into the Europe-is-a-Great-Thing approach, 'that those who oppose the motion want to remain with the past organisation of the nation state which brought about two world wars and mass genocide in Europe while those in favour want new forms of organisation which will have greater success'. This mouthful brought him victory by 493 votes to 92.

I'm surprised Peter Shore agreed to go back to the Oxford Union but, almost five years to the day, he did. This time he was opposed by the ever-lovely Shirley Williams and Geoffrey Rippon, proud inheritor of the Reginald Maudling Memorial Sleeping Bag. This is where I heard the Rippon 'one-way ticket to Siberia' line for the first time. I thought at first he said 'one-way ticket to Suburbia' and felt bound to agree, but I've heard him say it again twice and it *is* Siberia. Shirley Williams won for Europe convincingly enough, because, I think, everybody likes her even when she says things like, as she did on this occasion, 'Look beyond your living room. This country needs a vision.' She so obviously looks beyond her living room and clearly has visions; she probably hears voices too. She'd make a great Joan of Arc.

I fancy Peter Shore didn't win again because, although he's sharp as a tack, he is weaselish. I know that's terribly unfair but, nonetheless, painfully true. The Common Market was 'not a community', he said, 'but an organised bazaar', thumping the tub as he spoke. Great stuff, too, but he still looked weaselish. I don't know what we can do about it. I wish him nothing but well. Perhaps I shall send him a cutting from my beard.

The Result

Of the total electorate, which is what counts when the chips are down at the end of the day, 43.4 per cent voted 'Yes' and 21.1 per cent voted 'No'. The Western Isles and the Shetlands voted 'No', and no one can call them insular.

'It means', said Harold Wilson, 'that 14 years of national argument are over'. Mrs Thatcher said, 'It is really thrilling'. Both wrong.

Strange Medal Struck

The Pobjoy Mint struck a Harold Wilson medallion to celebrate the referendum. It was a tribute to the longest-serving Labour prime minister and pioneer of the referendum.

You could have one in solid platinum for as little as £295. Or a silver one for £12.50 – worth more today, one would imagine, but perhaps not. For £5.50 you could have him 'bronzed'. And fit, presumably. Hands up all those who have one. Aren't we an uncaring nation?

FRANCE

Another debate I caught in the same week as Peter Shore's second coming to the Oxford Union was organised by Thames Television and starred, yet again, Mr Geoffrey Rippon and, yes, the one-way ticket to Siberia. The motion was 'That the British are Bad Europeans', with which I would imagine few would disagree, but the gorge rose, the black bile bubbled, umbrella-handles were bitten through in a million homes when the proposer was introduced. A Frog, no less! Rivet, rivet. He should talk. He did.

If the Oxford Union is laid out loosely on the House of Commons principle, this debate seemed to be conducted in a court-room, and one could sense the nation's trauma at being arraigned before the beak by this obvious Gaullist. Geoffrey Rippon did a slow action replay of his Oxford speech, which was no defence in this case, reasserting that the Community was a wonderful thing offering permanent access to 250 million people, etc, and had nothing to do with our goodness or badness as Euro-persons.

Luckily, to enliven the proceedings, Thames Television had found a brace of right anti-Market ravers. There was a London taxi-driver who spoke loudly of the shed blood of his father and several other relatives as well, and of the war to end all wars, and of the Dunkirk spirit. There was also an air vice-marshal or such who clearly remembered Dresden even if you didn't, and pronounced grandly that we were quite the best of Europeans; in fact, we had proved it by twice smashing the wily boche, who jolly well ought to thank us very much and stop cringing. At this moment 12 red-bearded dwarfs entered and the court was momentarily cleared by Mr Justice Cocklecarrot (presiding). Old Father Thames in his wisdom had washed up the dynamic duo beside an earnest young German who, given their activities, was lucky to be there at all.

Sanity for the antis was provided by farming folk: a disgruntled farmer who complained bitterly about the Common Agricultural Policy and how the French had succeeded in making it their own, and a tight-lipped young lady apple-grower who had firm views on the Golden Obnoxious.

Let us therefore look at these two unacceptable faces of the Community.

Les Archeurs:
An Everyday Story of French Farming Folk

(Scene: a café in Ampont-sur-Am. An accordion is playing the theme music. Sound-effects of clinking glasses and bottles, *le table-football* being played, and finally of two men sitting down heavily for breakfast.)

Victor-Hugo Archeur: *'Allo. Bonjour, Daniel, et que voulez-vous pour le petit déjeuner?*

Daniel Archeur: *'Allo, Victor-Hugo, très gentil de vous. Un petit café au lait et une demi-tasse de Calvados, s'il vous plâit.*

Victor-Hugo (shouting): *'Allo, Jacques. Deux cafés au lait et beaucoup de Calvados. Eh, Daniel, comment ça va la ferme?*

Daniel Archeur: *Je ne peux complainer. Si nous faisons rien de tout un petit bourgeois vient de Bruxelles et me donne un sodding grand subside très gross indeed.*

Victor-Hugo (raising glass): *Vive la Policie Commun Agriculturelle! C'est la même chose avec moi! Je fais la FA dance, et ils me donnent une petite bleeding fortune.*

Jacques, le barman: *Bonjour, gentilhommes. Café et Calvados.*

Daniel Archeur: *Et, Jacques, pendant les moments que vous êtes at it, deux green drinks dégoûtants, s'il vous plâit. Nous sommes célébratant.*

RADIO TROIS — Les Archeurs

RADIO

Jacques: *Ça va la femme Daniel? Elle marche? La belle Peggy?*

Daniel: *Merci beaucoup pour demandant, Jacques. Elle est dans la puce. Elle a fait une grande effigie de Madame Thatcher. Nous étions up toute la nuit étouffant le great bag avec offal. Over le weekend nous l'exploderons au-dehors la mairie. Et votre femme fatale, Dorise?*

ON THE 28ᵀʰ APRIL LAST THIS WOMAN TRIED TO ROB 8 MILLION EUROPEAN FARMERS

SHE'S A DANGEROUS MOBSTER

MRS THATCHER

WANTED

50 000 E.C.U. REWARD

Victor-Hugo: *Un peu fatiguée, Daniel, à dire la verité. Toute last semaine elle a deposité turnips tout up et down la Route National Un. Et mon eldest, Gregoire, est down à Perpignan setting feu aux juggernauts espagnol.*

Daniel: *Aha, bien fait, Gregoire. Mon fils, Jean-Pierre, a été démonstratant à Londres no less au sujet de la sheepmeat et le refusal blunt de la Grande Bretagne sur les grounds de health à purchaser notre vieux lait. 'Allo, c'est Henri de Toulouse-Larkin.*

Henri de Toulouse-Larkin: *'Allo, mes vieux beauties!*

Victor-Hugo Archeur: *Deux grands cognacs pour Henri, Jacques!*

Henri de Toulouse-Larkin: *Daniel, mon vieux ravisseur de moutons, puis-je avoir un loan de votre tracteur?*

Daniel Archeur: *Hélas, Henri, mais mon neveu, Alfonse, porte les œufs et les tomates rotten à Bordeaux pour les jeter aux touristes britanniques. Pourquoi, Henri?*

Henri de Toulouse-Larkin: *Jethro et moi allaient à Paris pour plougher up le Wilton dans la bibliothèque de la British Embassy. Eh bien, zut alors!*

Victor-Hugo Archeur: *'Allo encore, ici le petit bourgeois de Bruxelles avec son sac de monnaie. Bonjour!*

Daniel Archeur: *Champagne, Jacques, pour Henri, Victor-Hugo et moi et, pour notre ami de Bruxelles, un delicious d'or.*

(Theme music comes up. Sounds of corks popping, the crunch of an apple being eaten, and a sound not unlike a jackpot being hit.)

The Apple War

Growing apples must have been a pleasant occupation. They are almost silent, don't trail through your kitchen with muddy hooves and you don't have to rise with the lark to plug their udders into the light-socket. (My brother-in-law, I remember, just north of the Pyrenees, came upon cork farming – an even more peaceful existence. You only have to harvest cork once every seven years, and in the meantime you just sit watching it grow.) Our apple-growers were a cheerful breed, and the fruit of their labours inspired me to song:

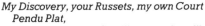

*Come wander thro' the orchards, when I've
    put my brand new suit on,
You're my pride of Kent, my flower of Kent,
    as fell on Isaac Newton,
You're my Cox's Orange Pippin (oh,
    Rosamund, that's nice!)
Fancy some Early Victoria Codlin and a
    little Darcy Spice?*

*Be my Bramley, be my Worcester, be my
    Beauty of Bath,
(There's an apple called an Irish Peach – it
    isn't right to laugh),
Be my Cornish Gillyflower, be my Cornish
    Aromatic,
Admire my Adam's Pearmain, and I shall
    be ecstatic!*

*My Discovery, your Russets, my own Court
    Pendu Plat,
Observe my Miller's Seedlings gently spill
    into my hat,
But I've you, my Blenheim Orange, so
    comely, so nutritious,
Unlike that nasty French thing, you're both
    golden and delicious.*

An Inspector from Brussels inspects a Golden Delicious and pronounces it Grade I.

There is the worm in the apple-core – the French Golden Delicious. Since we entered the Market in 1972 and the old protective quota system vanished, tons of the nasty frog-green things have poured into this country and, at the present rate, British producers will be hard-put to grow as many as are imported. The Golden Delicious could have been designed by the advertising men. Millions of tasteless clones of the original pour off the conveyor-belt: cheap! glossy! juicy! and long-lasting! You've seen the commercial where assorted persons chomp out *Frère Jacques* in F with their teeth on an apple. In 1979 the French paid £1 million to plug the Golden Delicious in Britain, and half of that million came from the French Government. Is it a coincidence that the Golden Delicious has featured heavily in the advertisements for those *Emmanuelle* movies over the years? No depths unplumbed.

Another problem is that, for 52 weeks of the year, there are Golden Delicious apples on the shelves – looking like wax fruit, but without the flavour – while the honest British apples, some facing extinction, tend to erupt at different seasons of the year. The Cox's Orange Pippin, for instance, only runs from early October to May. This brings them into line with Mother Nature, but not with Brussels. Suffice to say, Brussels in its wisdom favours the mass-produced large green apple* and, under regulations established prior to British entry, showers cash upon the happy French pomme-pedlar – cash for which our smaller, tastier apples do not qualify.

In 1979, five per cent of Britain's apple orchards, some 12,000 acres, were put to the bulldozer. Soon, presumably, they'll pull up all the orchards in Kent to widen the motorways for juggernaut-loads of green, Froggy apples. Such is the way of the new Old World.

The Golden Delicious leaves a very nasty taste in the mouth. See for yourself: eat one today! Conversely chomp out 'Cox's Orange Pippin' to the tune of *Land of Hope and Glory*. This happy task will cause your heart to sing.

* as it favours anything large and mass-produced.

A FASCINATING FRENCH COMPETITION

Correctly number these French kings and test your brain-power. Relations and employees of French kings may not enter.

Louis the Pious
Louis the Stammerer
Louis the Sluggard
Louis the Fat
Louis the Young
Louis the Lion
St Louis
Louis the Quarreller
Louis the Spider

Your personal rating
If you answered one out of ten correctly – that's quite good enough.
Two out of ten correct – quite unnecessary. Any more than that and you must be a relation or employee and are therefore subject to a steward's enquiry.

Holidaying in France

I was in the first-ever live transmission of a comedy show over the Eurovision network. We were fired from the front at Menton, between Monte Carlo and the Italian border, into several British homes. It was a bold notion conceived by Ned Sherrin, who also gave birth to *TW3*, and he assembled a motley gang of knock-abouts plus Cleo Laine plus French cameras and crew on what nautical folk refer to, I think, as a groin. I was first on, setting the tone, and was called upon to direct some poor lost Englishman to the park. I can't remember a word of it, but the gist was 'Past the Hotel Bristol, left at the Westminster, cross the Boulevard des Anglais by Barclays Bank, turn right at Cooks, left at the English church and it's behind the statue of Queen Victoria'.

The programme was called *An Englishman Abroad* and, while I represented the up-market Anglais, Ronnie Barker and Roy Kinnear symbolised the class two readership. We had been adopted by some visiting Welsh who sought to fortify us with Nut Brown Ale which they kept in the boot of their Morris. They had also brought several sacks of potatoes with them which they went into the hills to cook, thus avoiding the horrors of foreign cuisine. A golden moment was when Barker and Kinnear, in shirt-sleeves and braces and with handkerchiefs knotted about their heads, were rehearsing a Waterhouse/Hall sketch about North Country men abroad. They had reached a dramatic moment about discovering a Bass house, somewhere in Nice behind the Negresco, near that shop where you can buy those caddy spoons, when they were joined by a third party, a layman, similarly attired. He listened for a while and, finding the conversation of great interest, he interjected his own discovery of a bar that sold Watney's Red Barrel in Cannes. Barker and Kinnear stuck rigidly to the dialogue while our new-found friend embroidered it with the very stuff of life. Fiction and fact interwove contentedly. I only mention these incidents because the following morning's *Daily Express* ran a scathing piece saying that the Englishman abroad was in no wise similar to those depicted, and that the whole episode was a grotesque travesty of all we hold most often.

Le Camping

Le camping is something the French understand. They love to get under canvas, but they do also enjoy their comforts. So if you hit one of the larger sites (five red tepees in the *Michelin Guide* to camping spots) it will be as well-serviced as the best hotel, with swimming-pools, restaurants, bathrooms, etc, and all you provide is the room.

One cautionary tale: Hodges, a good friend of mine, was camping *en famille* near the Loire on a fairly pleasant one-star camping ground. At the end of the first week of his stay he noticed with alarm that the sign by the gate now boasted four stars, so he immediately repaired to the bureau to find if this meant that prices would rise accordingly. Reassured on this point, he enquired in a subtle manner as to the reasons for the camp site's sudden elevation. The cheery reply was 'No cholera this week!'

Le camping certainly makes it possible to tour *la belle France* in August without prior reservations. Our team set out in a Volkswagen Camper (a converted Dutch customs bus that had roamed the docks at Rotterdam, never, I think, moving above second gear) and while Brittany, Normandy and Aquitaine were full, we could usually find a corner of a field for the night. Every three days we'd move inland and stay at a hotel, but we enjoyed the odd communion with nature. I was aiming for an old stomping-ground – St Jean-Cap-Ferrat, beyond Nice – where, in the old days, you could spend a week *chez* Madame Robinson for £12 all found, leaving you with ample funds for a flutter at the wheel in Ian Fleming's favourite casino at Beaulieu. We never reached it because the traffic was intensely August and instead we spent four nights in Marseilles by the old harbour, which I can heartily recommend for those who like to live dangerously. Had we spent five nights there I wouldn't be here today, as the café we regularly patronised was visited that evening by Nemesis in the short, sharp shape of the local Cosa Nostra, who vented their spleen and several rounds of ammunition on the customers. *Très gai!*

Another cautionary note:

I once tried to check in at the Hotel de Dieu in Beaune. I thought the name was a little presumptuous until I was seen off by two laughing monks.

French Plumbing

During our various attempts at Common Market entry it was made clear that sacrifices would have to be made. Quite frankly, I thought that if E. Heath cared so deeply, the least he could have done was to volunteer to be first up on the Bardic slab, thus appeasing the gods in no uncertain manner. Then we would have been in a position to demand some reciprocal gesture from the French. What better, in my view, than that they should be obliged to bring their plumbing into line with the rest of the civilised world. A couple of footplates and a hole is not enough, and quartered copies of *Le Figaro* or *Maintenant!* nailed to the wall add nothing to the basic horror of the situation.

Imagine my surprise, therefore, when cricketing in Paris recently, at happening upon a new, thoroughly 1980s *pissoir* standing at the kerb somewhere near the Rue de Ravioli. It seemed at first to be a photo booth, but Charles Fry and I walked around it twice and assessed that it was a super-loo. Insert a franc, the instructions read, and at that a gleaming door slid open and Fry stepped in. Indeed as the door slid shut behind him, music welled up: this was certainly going to be an experience.

When Fry finally emerged (to the strains, incidentally, of *Sous les Ponts de Paris)* he held the door back and said generously 'Hop in'. I almost did. A franc a go seemed exorbitant. Thank heaven some natural distrust of the French caused me to draw back. As the door slid closed again, all hell broke loose. The great machine juddered with the shock of blasts of water within. This must be the *nettoyage* and *disinfectant automatique* as advertised. It went on for a good minute, playing havoc with my bladder. Finally it ceased and for a further franc I entered the bright capsule (to the strains, incidentally, of *La Mer*). It was brilliantly lit, the music was gay, and walls, ceiling and floor had been thoroughly sluiced. Had I been inside, I would have emerged edible. In the midst of all this Concorde-style technology, it was a little disappointing to see the traditional two footplates and a hole. What struck one most forcibly about this super-loo was the painfully slow turnover for potential clients. If a queue formed some would die *in extremis.* The old *pissoir,* green and rusting possibly, could house at least 27 at a time, and was free, even if you did have to provide your own music. (Extracts, incidentally, from *Les Parapluies de Cherbourg.)*

Monsieur Guy de Eaupassant, the great and, many would say, last French plumber, demonstrating his breakthrough in sanitary engineering to the court of the Sun King at Versailles. It is interesting to note that nothing has altered over the centuries since this prototype. The newspaper may be more recent.

A MOMENT OF TRUTH
ON *Newsnight*
RE THE NEW HEBRIDES

(Overheard on the night before an Anglo-French force was
meant to be going to the New Hebrides)

Charles Wheeler (BBC): Minister, they will be working together?
Peter Baker (Foreign Office): They have to work together.
   (Thoughtful pause)
Charles Wheeler (BBC): Hand in hand?
   (Further thoughtful pause)
Peter Baker (Foreign Office): Hand in hand.

One imagines that it was this interview, coupled with French
notions of *la vice anglaise* that caused their premature
withdrawal. Also, their traditional weakness against the bow
and arrow (see Agincourt, etc).

New Hebridean Fact:
Pidgin for brassière is 'Basket
him blong titties'.

Perfect Example of Disgraceful French Behaviour re EEC

A pedigree racehorse can be worth £200,000 and upwards these days and indeed is frequently snapped up for such a price. In Britain the 15 per cent VAT is tacked on, without an eye being batted. The wily Frog, however, has hit upon a brilliant trick (one would say 'con' but it translates rudely into the French). No matter what the actual value of the beast is, be it a Mill Reef or a Rhum Rouge, as far as they're concerned it is valued as a lump of dead horsemeat (see French Cuisine) and taxed on what it would fetch at the nearest abattoir. Thus, a couple of hundred thousand pounds changes hands, and the VAT is based on some £600.

The French, when threatened by the European Commission with an appearance before the European Court of Justice (Eurobeak), simply shrugged their shoulders in the Gallic manner and said that they were merely trying to rationalise the whole system. They maintained that the only time in a horse's life when you could value it with accuracy was when it was as stiff as a board, roast to a nicety, and placed on a silver salver at Maxim's with its legs in the air.

Even if forced to change their ways, they can still levy the VAT at whatever rate they choose, as it isn't necessary under EEC rules to have a blanket 15 per cent as we do.

On a more personal note, what the EEC happily refer to as 'liberal professions', such as painting, writing and acting, can be exempt from VAT. The French have convinced the EEC that racehorse training is a liberal profession and, as Brussels haven't in fact accurately defined the liberal professions, so it is. Rest assured that somewhere in Brussels 30 or 40 bureaucrats are working on it, and have been for years, but in the interests of job security, there's no point in coming up with an answer.

Q Does the same system work with the sale of dead footballers and, if so, how disgusting?

A Very – and jockey tastes better.

In the lee of the edible snail mountain, French gastronomes are cross-fertilising, like beavers and ants might if the mood so took them, in the hope of producing a horse with frog's legs. This would not only be a culinary wonder, but would be worth a fiver each way in the Grand National.

Recent exchange in sordid Parisian Bar

Rushton: *Une bière, s'il vous plâit.*
La patronne: *Oui, m'sieu.*
Doxy: *I will drink champagne with you for 400 francs.*
Rushton: *It will cost you a deal more than that, dear.*

'Frenchman helped in Piltdown Man hoax'

FURTHER EXAMPLE OF GALLIC DEVIOUSNESS

A Brisk Question and Answer Session

Q What do the French think of us?

A Here one can most easily gauge international feelings by studying their jokes. In French jokes about the British, we seem to emerge as suave pederasts, certainly sexual deviants, but always cool as cucumbers. A classic is of the Englishman whose wife dies, while holidaying on the Riviera. A funeral is arranged, and the widower goes into Cannes for a black hat. (At this stage I must remind you that the French for 'French letter' is not *belle lettre française* but, justifiably you may think, *capeau anglais*. You won't need reminding that the French for 'hat' is *chapeau*.) *'Avez-vous'*, he enquires of a shop assistant, *'un capeau noir?'* (I didn't say it was a good joke.) *'Pourquoi, m'sieur?'*, enquires the shop-assistant. *'Pourquoi noir?' 'Ma femme'*, replies the recently bereaved, *'est morte'. 'Ah les Anglais!'* is the cheery punch line, *'quelle delicatesse!'* There you see we emerge with some credit from a necrophilic yarn.

NECROPHILIC YAWN

Q What do they do well?

A Eat, drink and ride the bicycle for long distances. They make the best films. They used to paint wonderfully well and wrote good songs before the war. I'm afraid I'm not an admirer of Jacques Brel who has reduced the love song to such banalities as:

'I must empty the waste-paper basket!
I must hoover the cat.
Put a new light-bulb in the bedside lamp.
Change the pillow-cases.
Marie is coming up the stairs.'

This is delivered standing with one's legs wide apart, exuding increasing panic and tremolo as she nears. Charles Aznavour is another with a boring tale to sing. He spends a lot of time dancing alone in an empty kitchen. I have heard it suggested that the diminutive Froggy's lot would improve were he to kiss a princess.

Q What do you think of the *Comédie Française?*

A It is a serious business.

Q How do tall French presidents cope?

A God only knows.

M. DISCARD GITANES

AND HIS LOVELY WIFE VALERY

AFTER M. PONTY

Q What are the French up to?

A Up to about five foot eight inches (0.00073 of a kilometre, if you must). At this point they invariably stop, except for certain rugby forwards, specially bred in the Pyrenees, and presidents. De Gaulle was very tall, Giscard got the job entirely from the 'tallest on the Right theory', and Monsieur Pompidou slipped through by standing on a crate of Mouton Rothschild '57 behind a very tall wife. Ask me another.

Q You bushy-faced buffoon, what are they up to in the Common Market?

A No good. A centuries-old French posture. As we have seen, concussed by war, they entered the Market like sheep-meat, or *moutons* as they have it, but as their natural arrogance re-emerged under their first tall president since the hostilities, of a sudden it was Halle de la Liberté, sod Egalité and you can *oublier* la Fraternité. Cynics will say that the *Marché Commun* is the result of a Franco-German plot conceived by those two grand old crooks, Adenaueur and De Gaulle. The cynics are probably right. The French, having fallen into the pit, theatrically speaking, were eager to get their act back on the world stage and the Germans saw that such an alliance would (a) have them back on a business footing in a nonce, and would (b) protect them from their worst enemy, themselves. The French and the Germans are, of course, still at it. One of the more jovial ironies is that, when Giscard and Schmidt meet in public, Giscard will hazard a little German, *'lieber Helmut'* and the like, and Schmidt will respond with a little French. The moment they get behind closed doors, they both relax into English which they speak fluently. Ho! Ho! Ho!

Catching the Judge's Eye

Pictured here are the finalists in an annual Charles de Gaulle look-alike contest. The judges will be looking for size, shape, a long nose, a hint of megalomania, a mistrust of the British, an intense dislike of the Americans and good arm movements. The entry is always large for there is no political party in France, including the Communists, who do not firmly believe that they are carrying the torch of Gaullism. This year, as usual, the prize – having a Parisian street named after you – was not awarded.

WEST GERMANY

To tell the truth, the Germans, given their behaviour, shouldn't be coming out till about 1993. Rudolph Hess has done time 30 years longer than they have. Their record is appalling: grievous bodily harm, robbery with intent, riotous assemblies, behaviour likely to, terminal mugging, carrying offensive weapons, vandalism, murder in the first degree, and the second degree, and even the Three Degrees would have been at risk. (Marry them, Charlie Windsor, and perk us up no end!)

Forgive and forget, you may say. Look at them now, they're going straight. But the fact of the matter is, they tried to kill me when I was little. One has to draw the line somewhere.

Here's a grand old joke, stiff with meaning, from the good old days of the Establishment Club:

Lord Home (being interviewed): Damned clever, the Germans; that's why they won the war.
Interviewer: They didn't win the war, Foreign Secretary.
Lord Home: In the long run.

No one is more conscious that the Germans are still on probation than Herr Schmidt and, while the temptation must ever be lurking to seize the lead in Europe, tomorrow the world – and with

his qualifications he is actively encouraged to do so – he knows he mustn't. As he frequently puts it, the softer the Germans tread, then the sooner Auschwitz will be forgotten. What he can do, however, is trip down the same avenue with President Giscard. It's a very useful relationship. For instance, whatever Schmidt thinks of the American leadership, he must be seen to uphold the American connection, while Giscard, to keep the Gaullist tradition going, must be seen not to. Thus, Schmidt can go to Moscow despite American disapproval, and Giscard can go there regardless. Schmidt, however, can support America by boycotting the Olympic Games, while Giscard certainly can't. The one person who won't join in on any of these ventures is Mother Thatcher. If she went to Moscow, it would be lead for Britain, and not off the roof of St Basil's. She's best left at home, whitewashing the windows, wrapping herself in brown paper and sharpening her US-made cutlery. She's been in the dog-house, anyway, ever since Britain's un-European activities re the Budget and the CAP. As any good breeder will tell you, when you're seeking to amaze the world with a cross between a poodle and a dachshund, the last thing you need around is a rabid bulldog.

Therefore any talk of a sharp rise in Europe's world influence can be put down to, firstly, America's sharp decline and, secondly, France

and Germany grasping the nettle, and stirring with it. All this causes stifled squeals of glee from the Kremlin. In their perfect world Europe would be neutral, but ignoring American stratagems and going their own sweet Euro-way is quite good.

Hamburg Revisited

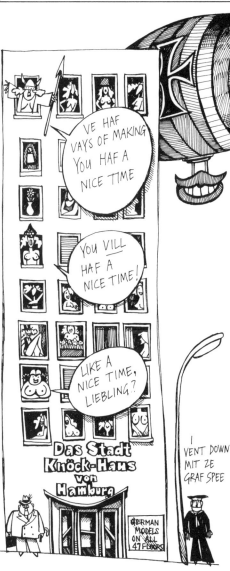

VE HAF VAYS OF MAKING YOU HAF A NICE TIME

YOU VILL HAF A NICE TIME!

LIKE A NICE TIME, LIEBLING?

Das Stadt Knöck-Haus von Hamburg

GERMAN MODELS ON ALL 47 FLOORS

I VENT DOWN MIT ZE GRAF SPEE

One of my clearer memories of national service (and, in fairness, I was barracked between a brewery and a cigar factory so memories are clearly dim), is the local Anglo-German Society, or Anglo-Kraut Klub as we knew it, which was formed to improve relations between the army of occupation and the local Westphalians. It was there that young, blond Aryans would cry 'Next time!' and, imitating the sound of a souped-up Stuka, would pretend to machine-gun us with both fists juddering.

There's never been any doubt in my mind that the Germans take their pleasures sadly. Conversely, of course, they'll laugh like hyenas at someone breaking a leg, but when it comes to being on pleasure bent – and bent is the word, particularly where their pleasures are concerned – they're as merry as chiropodists or windscreen-wiper salesmen. I saw this for myself in 1955 when I went north to Hamburg on a WVS-sponsored dirty weekend pass. There were four of us, all eager to learn what was never taught in those days, although admittedly I knew precisely what birds do to bees and vice versa. Naturally we gravitated briskly to the Reeperbahn: the Wembley, we were told, of all-lady nude mud-wrestling. The season, however, appeared to be over. Either that or the war had pruned their slithery ranks. A fearsome experience it must have been for Tommy to be thrust suddenly into a cross-buttock by a bare Brunhilde in a wet trench.

My word, how the memories come flooding back through the cigar-smoke and the gassy beer. The Winkelstrasse, blocked and forbidden to members of HM Forces by metal screens, was strangely reminiscent of the Burlington Arcade save that, instead of every window sporting tourist-grabbing cashmere cardigans and nasty china objects, in each of these windows sat a large lady. There wasn't a lard mountain in those days, but these ladies were a living personification of one. Indeed, to have mounted one would certainly have required oxygen and a team of Sherpas.

Occasionally, potential customers, usually tiny men in pale grey, crêpe-soled shoes, would press their faces to the glass and wave. The lady in question would then open negotiations by spelling out her charges on podgy fingers. The client would either shake his head vigorously and move on, or spell out on the steamy glass a more reasonable sum. This soundless haggling would continue until the gloomy little hedonist either sought postures new or vanished inside, never, to my knowledge and not in the circumstances surprisingly, to be seen again.

I recall a vast beer house full of smoke and earnest, elderly married couples seeking perhaps to recapture the equally tatty and depressing moments of their youth. To the dank strains of a small, military band, a buxom fraulein in a corset would march to the centre of the stage and, accompanied by the rhythmic clapping of the assembled Jerry-atrics and the martial thump of the bass drum, would jump up and down on the spot at attention. The *moment suprême* which set the congregation on Das Buzz came later when, while still in mid-air, the danseuse violently and unceremoniously ripped open the front of her corsetry, causing two huge breasts to burst onto the scene like a dead-heat in a Zeppelin race. Tassels, which hung like anchor-chains, slowly began to revolve. 'Oh, the humanity! Oh, the people!' one was tempted to cry. If just one of those Hindenbergs collided with one of the customers, the whole evening might perk up considerably.

However, I digress. Back at the Reeperbahn, my companions had disappeared. My lapels were seized by the white gloves of one of the many commissionaires that line the Street of a Thousand Clip-joints. He nearly had me over several times as he enthusiastically mimed for me the speciality of the house. I fought him off. I was lost and friendless in the Reeperbahn, and I had to run the gauntlet of uniformed touts. My enquiry for three men in tweeds caused a panic in the market-place. My bizarre request was passed up and down the line: it clearly stretched their resources. I was offered Lascars in *lederhosen,* Westphalians in wet-suits, and even boys from Brazil. I fled.

I found the others eventually after a lurid search in a *nachterie.* My comrades-in-arms were gathered on an upper floor in front of a rude screen on which cavorted – not exactly in technicolour, for I fancy they'd been hand-tinted – three gentlemen, a lady and an Alsatian dog. It was difficult to work out precisely what was happening on the screen, though Barbara Woodhouse might have made a more educated guess. I thought, perhaps, some of the gentlemen had lost their contact-lenses, but when I saw where they were all searching, that seemed to be stretching coincidence too far. Again, possibly they were all blind, but then so apparently was their guide-dog, who had an appalling sense of direction.

I was nearly at the steps leading up to the lads when the screen parted. The Alsatian split asunder. The lady's legs cracked apart like a wishbone. 'Keats', I said, superstitiously. Through the gap, live and in living colour, marched another corseted Amazon. If Hitler had slapped one of these maidens on every rock on the Rhine, we'd never have crossed it. She, however, was about to cross me: I lay directly in her path. I flattened myself against a customer and she missed by inches. I scuttled to our table. The screen was now showing a Laurel and Hardy film. I kept expecting Stan to mount Oliver, or kiss Hardy, but it was the incongruous piano-moving scene and, while one would not have expected to find them on the bill at the Odeon, Sodom, we laughed uproariously until we were ejected for disturbing the peace.

Now, I gather, much of Hamburg's grotty

gaiety has come under State control. There are 50-storey bordellos, spick as Holiday Inns and span as morgues. The ponce has given way to the chairman of the board.

Not a relaxed society

My word, I was happy to see this headline in a *Times* special report on West Germany. The very phrase that had been trembling on my lips since I first fell among them in 1957. I'd been struck by their formality in the orderly room, when I was leave clerk and second-in-command of Sixth Armoured Division. There were two of us disbanding it, and my colleague, being the senior acting-unpaid-lance-corporal by a fortnight, was naturally in command. We kept the Division alive far longer than had been anticipated, and as it contained only the pair of us, there were benefits.

For one thing, I organised extensive leaves. Working with us in the orderly room were a couple of German civilians: benign old Frau Wolf who typed electrically before the electric typewriter, and Herr Cornelius, an enormous man who refused to discuss the war and wore large grey brothel-creepers. We imagined the reason his great shoes were soled and heeled in solid crêpe, like those of so many of his countrymen, was to deaden the sound as he automatically clicked his heels when the CO came in. Herr Cornelius viewed us with undisguised contempt. We were given to wearing bedroom slippers on duty and invariably sat with our tunics open, waving fat cigars while concocting feeble excuses to the RSM about lost files. One felt that he had been part of a military machine that had been unable to relax. The truth was too horrible for him to bear. He was able to muster some comfort from a stiff, formal relationship with Frau Wolf, but with us he was lost.

This apparently is the case today in German business circles. No Christian names there: 'Herr Doktor' and 'Frau' are the order of the day.

They outnumber simple 'Herrs' and there aren't many 'Frauleins'. To preserve their sanity the office party is total bacchanalia, but the following morning sees the poker once more rammed up the trousers, and the wild blonde tresses of the previous eve knotted and glued to the skull once more.

I remember one field-grey day in John le Carré weather, which is the worst weather in fiction since Shakespeare, with snow and ice as cold as a Tory manifesto, when the Regiment marched down into the town while the band played. (It was a Tank Regiment and I'm happy to recall that the regimental march was *It Wasn't the Yanks that Won the War, It was My Boy Willie.*) The locals poured out of their homes on hearing the sounds of brass and drum and marching feet. Unfortunately, on icy cobble and a sharp downhill slope, the marching feet would vanish from under us, and we would fall with infinitely more drama than a fainting guardsman. The Germans watched in baleful silence, torn probably between laughter and tears. Not a relaxed society.

BELGIUM

'I would rather trust a Fleming with my butter':
Merry Wives of Windsor.

In the same way that 'Bloody Belgians!' has become the anguished cry of the enraged motorist on the roads of Europe, so 'Bloody Brussels!' has become the instant riposte to the ever-increasing lunacies of the criminally inane of the EEC. No more suitable place could have been selected for their headquarters.

The old adage that, had a committee sat on the basic design for the horse it would finally have come up with the camel, goes out of the window in Brussels. There, by the time the ground-plan for the Euro-horse had passed through the system, the final product would be more akin to a hairy mammoth with one leg.

Let's take a gentle stroll down the endless Brussels corridors where every door is sprayed with letters as if a chimpanzee had been let loose with a John Bull printing set. Let us see if we can find an isle of sanity in Kafkaville.

A Brussels Notebook

(Overheard in a corridor of power)
Bureaucrat: I am an initiator of programmes.
Another: What sort of things do you initiate?
Bureaucrat: Programmes.

In Brussels we find a senior official, a £12,000-a-year man (with Euro-perks). His secretary's sole duty, prior to the admission of Britain, Eire and Denmark, was to provide him daily with six freshly-sharpened coloured pencils. With these he would carefully draw the flags of the six member nations. On the admission of the further three countries, his secretary's duties extended to providing and sharpening nine coloured pencils. At the end of every working day the flags were fed into the shredder.

Hanging over his head like the Sword of Damocles is the prospect of Greek, Spanish and Portuguese entry. Will there be sufficient time in a day to draw a dozen flags? How many more coloured pencils must be indented for? Can the shredder cope? How long, dear Lord, how long? You will find him under either 'Centralised Information Activity' in the book, or any good-sized stone.

Under the Commission, there are 20-odd directorates-general. You can forget all the free, open-market crapola: each country jealously guards its posts and hands them on to fellow-countrymen. Nationality is the first consideration, with qualifications a poor second. Like the other eight, the British insist on their fair share, from the four director-generals to the full whack of 80 British chauffeurs. The Agricultural Commission is always French.

I know a charming ex-Euro-person who, on the first day in his enormous office, was asked by his secretary if he wanted 'Everything or nothing?' Rather foolishly, but keen as mustard, he said 'Everything'. On the following morning he could hardly force open the door of his office for bundles of paper and documents. After that he said 'Nothing' and was equally as wise.

If you are a secretary with a degree you qualify for an 'A' job. You can't, however, get a

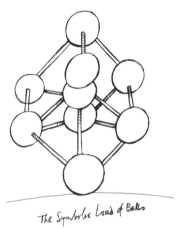

The Symbolic Load of Balls

'B' job as this is for those without degrees. This rule does not apply to 'C' jobs, so there are a number of chauffeurs with PhDs. British girls, lured to Brussels by the high salaries, the holidays, the two-hour lunch-breaks, and the low income tax, invariably go mad from loneliness or constant calorie-packed Belgian gateaux or worse, too many foreigners, simply for something to do.

Civil servants get the best deal. They can earn twice as much at Berlaimont, and their perks include child benefits, living-in-Brussels benefits, not-living-at-home benefits, and holiday travel allowances. In addition, they're paid in Euro-money which is worth five per cent more than Belgian currency. They pay very little tax and live the life of Riley. The unpaid bills in the bureaucrats' restaurants form another mountain, and they work their way through the hospitality budget like cockroaches.

My friend's children were at a comprehensive school in London, but the EEC insisted on paying him an education allowance. His eldest was studying geology and, as the EEC school didn't cover this, they allowed him a further back-hander.

Happy Euro-tale

My friend was in the television, radio and films division of the Commission. He was instructed to make a film and was allotted a budget of £25,000 to do so. 'There's one thing to remember', said a British commissioner. 'For a number of reasons – all of them political – use a Danish director and crew.' As a matter of form, tenders were put out around the Nine, but my friend dutifully found a suitable gang of Danes and, giving them the £25,000, he léft them to get on with it. He then received a summons to appear before the CCMA, a watch-dog committee with representatives from each of the nine countries, whose usual role is to enquire into typewriting costs over £6,000. The committee seemed thoroughly irked.

'Did you', asked the German member, 'approach a German director?'

'Yes', my friend replied.

The German member persisted. 'Was he not good enough?'

'He was excellent', was the response.

'You approached, I trust', said the French member in French, 'a French director?'

'An excellent man with all the qualifications', answered my friend.

The committee members all nodded wisely, voted him out of order, and he was, of a sudden, £25,000 down the drain and sweating profusely.

'Appeal!' was the general advice offered. One of the first rules he'd learnt in Brussels was: never reveal your knowledge of, or abilities in, other languages. Apart from anything else, you enjoy the interpretations more. (I read of a splendid case of an Englishman telling a joke, through an interpreter, to a number of Danes. Quite a lengthy joke, it seemed to translate very quickly, but set them on the roar nevertheless. It was later revealed that the Danish interpreter hadn't understood a word of the joke, but had told his audience to clasp their sides and bellow on the command 'Three!', thus sealing the ties that bind.) Back my friend went to the committee to put his case. 'May I put it in English?', he asked politely. 'My French is not, alas, sufficient to handle the nuances of my submission.' This they allowed, and he embarked on a load of gobbledygook at the speed of a Sotheby's auctioneer. They listened to him in sheer bewilderment and, when he'd screeched to a halt, put their heads together for a judgement.

'*Raisonnable*', pronounced the chairman, and all was well.

No VAT News is Good News

Belgian VAT - Paras drop on an unsuspecting Shopping Area in Bruges in a Dawn Raid.

I suppose VAT was our first inkling of the shape of things to come. Some six weeks before its introduction I was telephoned by a customs and excise man. Could he come and see me? he wondered. He was in the anti-showbusiness platoon, whose offices, ironically, were off Shaftesbury Avenue, the heart of theatreland. He wanted, he said, to explain VAT and its workings to me. Gracious to a fault, I told him to come round any old time and, knowing he was coming, set about baking a cake.

He was not a happy man. A month before, he moaned, he had been happily ensconced in the 'nothing to declare' section at Heathrow. A contented lifetime of sniffing at the occasional rucksack lay before him, with a pension at the end of it. All this had been shattered by his call to the front. He showed me the green quarterly form and tried to explain input and output to me. I couldn't help feeling, at that stage, that the translator was at fault and that it probably made much more sense in the original Walloon. He showed me how to divide my life's work into columns and how to do invoices and demand receipts. I kept saying 'Yes' and 'No' alternately, a trick I'd picked up from Winnie-the-Pooh.

Feeling ultimately, as Pooh did with Owl, that it was time I asked something of the VAT man, I enquired about the position of my agent who was not registered with VAT, and whether he now got eight per cent of ten per cent, or ten per cent of eight per cent, and did I add it or subtract it, and was it input or output? He spoke longingly of days at London Airport, and said he would send a book* to help me.

Within 18 months, I was 15 months behind with my VAT, and received a brisk note saying that I would be visited by an inspector, whose name was something like Krakpolavitch. It certainly sounded like something from the roll-call shouted by a US Marine sergeant on the beach at Iwo Jima: Schultz! Dobermann! Skullbent! Cabanossi! O'Hara! Wittgenstein! Nijinsky! Brecht! Pavlova! Krakpolavitch! The appointment was arranged for 10 o'clock – in the morning, I hoped, but their hours are uncertain. The appointment could well have consisted of a hand-grenade through the letter-box in the night, and excise men pouring through the window with socks on their heads.

She was quite lovely. She moved with animal grace, clad in the graceful fur of some dead animal. It was Ms Krakpolavitch, no less. I drowned in the limpid pools of her deep brown eyes as they danced like a frog-pond in the rain over the rude hieroglyphics of my figures. Instead of freezing into a snarl, her full, red lips broke into a soft smile as she corrected my pathetic mathematics. She might have been reading a little Keats. From the innards of her Gucci bag she produced a pocket-computer, and sorted me out in one of the happiest hours of my life. Not since a Montague fell for a Capulet has a more ludicrous love blossomed. She a VAT woman, and I not at all. I realise it was one-sided now, but I got months behind again in the hope of another visit. Her perfume still lingered in my invoice book.

After a year, another visit was announced. My heart leapt like an okapi, but Ms Krakpolavitch didn't materialise. In her place came three heavies with bulging breast-pockets. One was very heavy, and the other two came, they said, for a bit of a laugh. There are those probably who joined the Waffen-SS for the same love of a good titter. The one who hadn't come to enjoy himself, clearly their leader, looked at my collected works with clenched teeth. Occasionally, he hummed the theme from *The Untouchables*. 'You'd better sort yourself out quickly', he grated.

'Yes', I said, getting a laugh from the lads. They were a good audience: they'd fallen about at my nervous 'Good morning'.

'I'm telling you this for your own good', he snarled. He narrowed his eyes, and shifted his briefcase meaningfully.

'Belgians!' I hissed after them, as the door slammed in their wake.

Apparently there's quite a high suicide rate within the ranks of the VAT men. The preferred method, if my informant is to be believed, is the closed garage door, the car-engine running and the final output, like Audrey Hepburn in *Sabrina Fair*. VAT can seriously damage your health.

* A child's guide, I hoped. I've said it before: there's very little to be said for anything that can't be explained to children. 'I will send you a reliable guide', he'd said. It arrived some days later: VAT for Florists.

The Euro-egg and I

APPENDIX II

EEC MARKETING STANDARDS FOR EGGS

QUALITY STANDARDS FOR EGGS OF CLASSES A B AND C

	CLASS A	CLASS B	CLASS C
Shell and membrane	Normal, clean, intact	Normal, intact	May be visibly cracked
Air cell	Not exceeding 6mm in depth, stationary	Not exceeding 9mm in depth	Not exceeding 9mm for incubator clears. (See also Appendix III 1e)
Egg White	Clear, translucent, of a gelatinous consistency, free of foreign substances of any kind	Clear, translucent, free of foreign substances of any kind	Class C includes all eggs which do not satisfy the requirements of Classes A and B but are suitable for the manufacture of foodstuffs for human consumption
Yolk	Visible under candling as a shadow only, without apparent contour, not moving perceptibly from its central position when the egg is rotated, and free of foreign substances of any kind	Visible under candling as a shadow only (although this is not required with eggs preserved in lime), and free of foreign substances of any kind	
Embryo	No perceptible development		Permitted
Smell	Free of all foreign odours		
Wet or dry-cleaning	Not permitted	Permitted	

All eggs which do not fall into Classes A B or C are classed as "Industrial Eggs" and may not be used for human consumption, either in the manufacture of foodstuffs or otherwise.

There was excitement in geological and geographical circles in July 1980, strange rumblings were apparent on the Richter Scale, and the birds stopped singing. North of the Butter Mountain and the River Lard, and to the south of Mont Bœuf and the Lac du Vin, the Egg Mountain is now emerging. Will it burst, lightly boiled or scrambled, from the bowels of the earth, or will it rise in more stately fashion like a soufflé? Opinions are divided.

Whereas in Holland and France you can buy half-a-dozen eggs for 18 pence or so (Size Four that is, Standard as was), in the UK they'll set you back 26 pence. (I realise that, by the time you read this book, these prices may seem like the egg salad days, and may, as you are now bartering your wife for a Size Six, cause you to burst into tears at the memory of these times. As I now write, 26 pence for half-a-dozen seems to stick.) Given the price of eggs on this side of the Channel, eager Dutch and Froggy farmers begin to whip their chickens into action. The Belgians are at it too, and Euro-eggs are hurtling into Britain at the rate of a million or so a week. This is suddenly where the money lies. As a result, egg prices fall, and it's œuf all over the faces of the British egg-men. 'I am the Egg-man! I am a Walrus!' they sing bitterly.

Dear ZiR.

Wot size EGG do you take??? Ha! Ha! Hollo laughter

You may think that being broot into line with the rest of EURUP is all your Xmasses in one basket but you are no chicken, cock. Have you seen the Regulashuns? (SORRY)

2. The Community has made three regulations on Marketing Standards for eggs. These are No. 1619/68, No. 95/69 and No. 1295/70. A translation of No. 1619/68 is available from HMSO*.

You should of bin here when that Chicken-shit hit the Battery!! That bluddy Rooster again. Pardon my French and RITING.

COP THIS

WHAT!!

Class A

13. The standards required for Class A eggs are almost identical to those required for "first quality" eggs. However the following points should be noted:

(i) fine shell cracks which are not visible to the naked eye are not regarded as faults*.

* But it should be noted that eggs with shell cracks will not be eligible for subsidy, whether or not the crack is visible to the naked eye.

The ITALICS are my own.

We all got koppies. Cluck! Cluck! Cluck! And have you klocked the new shapes.?

Weight Grades 1-7	Appropriate number 2-3 mm high not necessarily inserted in the triangle	△ 1 or △ 1

and | ◇ 1 or ◇ 1 | *and* | ★ Colour: Red |

stuff that for a lark!!

It's hard enough passing a Size 5 !!

Aggreeved HEN

IRELAND

The geographical centre of Ireland is Shannonbridge and, about 10 years ago, I spent a week there working on a 'fillum'. I played the part of a black-hearted Black Country villain, no less, who was beastly to children and was called Cromwell to add to his unpleasantness. If you had to explain Ireland hurriedly to an inquisitive Martian, Shannonbridge might well be the place to take him.

On the bank opposite the town, for starters, is an extraordinary relic: a British Army-built fortress, dating from the Napoleonic Wars. It was cunningly disguised as a row of cottages, but was built with such strange angles and extraordinarily warped perspectives that it would have appeared less massive when approached from the river by the French fleet that was anticipated.

First on the right as you come into Shannonbridge is the newish police station. The old police station, a three-storey building, is bang in the middle of Shannonbridge but, as a result of a bang in the middle of Shannonbridge in 1922, it is now an elegant ruin with a tree growing through the middle of it. The walls are still solid and it could have been turned into something else years ago, but that would have been an un-Irish activity.

Next to its successor is the town's second pub, which is run by the only Protestant for some miles around. To prove that there is no discrimination whatsoever, everybody drinks there at lunch-time. The populace waits outside patiently for as long as an hour after opening-time, watching mine host slowly approach up the main street, prodding his three cows home.

Carry on down the main street, and you will come to the birthplaces of Shannonbridge's two favourite sons: 'Legs' Diamond and, next door, George Murphy, who went to Hollywood and became a sort of Second Eleven Fred Astaire and then did a Ronald Reagan by becoming a Californian senator. Their photographs are proudly displayed in the number one pub, a rollicking spot, run by the Killeen family. As is traditional, apart from purveying song and Guinness, the pub also serves as a post office and general store. I can remember standing in the shop, clutching a pint of stout, and admiring the display of shrouds.

As you leave Shannonbridge you will see its largest building, the huge, modern Roman Catholic church, on your right. There you are, Martian visitor, it's all there, quaint and gently reminiscent of Hollywood, for you to see in microcosm. Sure, and isn't that John Wayne in a cloth cap going 15 rounds with Victor McClagen to the strains of *If You're Irish, Come into the Parlour?*

A literary outing on the Elysian Fields. Seen here with Samuel Beckett, James Joyce, Oscar Wilde, G.B.S. and Brendan-the-all-too-Human-Behan, is Patrick James Joyce O'Booze (called James after his father, Joyce after his mother), a Kerryman, and constant butt of their cheery quips.

Wine, Women and Song

History, said Stephen Daedalus, is a nightmare from which I am trying to awake. It's one thing to have a keen sense of history but, when you've heard Orangemen celebrating the Battle of the Boyne for the umpteenth time through their noses or if you've sat in some Galway bar and been assaulted with 47 choruses of *Oh, the Tommies Raped me Granny in 1922* or such, surely the time has come to stand up and cry 'Forget it!' While you're at it you could throw in a rider that they might all take their religion a lot less seriously, except for those whose behaviour suggests that they would benefit, as would the rest of us, from their taking religion a deal *more* seriously.

A Paddy called Paddy, would you believe, was a driver on the 'fillum' I mentioned earlier, and he fancied himself as something of a singer. There was nothing he liked more than to get up on a stage, stand rigidly at attention, stick his right hand in his right ear and, accompanied only by the stomping of one foot, give voice to *The Old Triangle*.

'I know a place', he said. Recommendation enough, we went. The place lay some 20 miles south of Dublin and seemed at first to be a tiny pub. We had a pint of Guinness each at the small, quiet bar and then, with his Irish eyes a-smiling – usually my cue to exit or duck – he led me through a small door.

There sat 300 Irishmen with yellow-green grins and ping-pong ball eyes, like Muppets stored in a cupboard. The music soared and scraped about them. Patriotic ditties recalling Granny's undoing in 1922 and such choruses as 'Ho. we're off to Dublin in the morn, in the morn, t'bayonets glistening in t'sun, ti-pom-ti-pom-ti-

pom and t'rattle of the Thompson gun' were interspersed with impassioned renderings of *Till* and *Release Me*. Someone shouted and banged his way through *The Old Triangle* twice. It was hell, until Arthur's Black Liffey Water began to work and then, just as I was beginning to warm to the frantic fiddling and the Engelbert O'Humperdincks, there were screams and crashes from the small, quiet bar beyond. An Irishman quickly bolted the door on our side and the bands played on. I was now carried away on the wings of melody. I sang with enthusiasm about the iniquitous behaviour of the Black and Tans and the absentee landlords, warbled movingly about the post office and the Easter Rising, and loftily bellowed the praises of the Irish Republican Army.

Paddy and I were the first to leave. The door was unlocked for us, and revealed was a scene of gory devastation. The small, quiet bar was a ruin of its former self: blood, glass, broken bottles and fragments of furniture littered the floor. I reasoned that, even with an Engelbert at full throttle, we would surely have heard a bomb. Paddy enquired of a white-faced, shaking barman what had occurred. 'T'was t'Dobblin whimmin, sorr', he said in dark green.

It transpired that a charabanc-load of dreaded Dublin women had arrived in search of resuscitation on their way home from an outing. The local Amazons had taken a dim view of their visitors, and the fur began to fly. How sensible that gentleman who slid the bolt.

When the film was over, Paddy refused a tip, but asked for contraceptive devices in lieu. I had Harrods make up a box for him.

The House Whine

I was once having dinner in one of Dublin's distinguished four-star hotels and, as is my wont at such times, was eavesdropping shamelessly. At the next table sat an American couple: affably loud, and probably touring around looking for ancestors. The interesting thing about Americans is that, having established that they're American, in next to no time they will proceed to fill you in on their Irish, Polish, Italian or Greek antecedents, and may even toss in bits of the relevant language for good measure. I imagine we'll be the same when *we're* united states.

The husband hailed the wine waiter. I reckon he had probably once been a jockey but had been eternally suspended for drunken driving during the Irish Sweeps Derby.

'My wife and I', vouchsafed the American, 'have been touring Europe, and at all our ports of call we have asked the wine waiter to bring us the *local* wine, the wine of the region. We have found this a most satisfying exercise and I should be grateful if you would select something suitable from your cellars. Some van d'you pay?'

The wine waiter recoiled, scratched his head and said 'Ah' in Irish. 'Well, now', he added. Then he looked hard and long at the wine list. 'Righty ho, sorr', he said, then hid behind a pillar for a while. He returned after about five minutes with two wine-glasses.

'Whine of t'country, is it then?', he said with a smile, and vanished again.

Finally he arrived with a rattling ice-bucket and, wrapped most properly in a napkin, a pint bottle of Guinness. He poured a little into the American's wine-glass and stood back, beaming.

Excuse me, sorr, but de Oirish in me's coming out again

No Irish Jokes

is Good for you

Oh, Bless me, Father, for Oi have sinned...

If the EEC is intended to purvey lasting peace then what, you will quite rightly enquire, of The Troubles? Not that one would care to see Panzers or French paras on the battered streets of Belfast, any more than one cares to see our own troops there. Perhaps the Vatican Guard in full-dress Michaelangelos, with Leonardo-designed road-blocks would be acceptable, but they would give Mr Paisley palpitations that would register on the Richter Scale.

It's painfully simple to lie Ireland on the couch and diagnose schizophrenia, brought on by excessive history, myth, religion and acts of parliament. However, you'd be torn too if the world at large – and your cousins across the water in particular – expected you to be quaint and gnomic, full of jigs, song, racing-tips and black drink on one hand and, on the other, expected you to be a hard-faced patriot in dark glasses with a service revolver in the pocket of your mackintosh. Either can be fatal. Far too many Irish have died too young from the sheer effort of being seen to be Irish. Perhaps it's all summed up in the contradictory nature of the wake.

Don't ask me why, but when I think of Ireland nowadays, I see earnest committees in Boston and New York raising funds to provide tiny Armalite rifles for leprechauns.

ITALY

Amidst all the concern about Venice sinking slowly into the fish soup that abounds in that region, the fact that the rest of Italy is descending rapidly into the sub-basement seems to be overlooked. Our own 'Thirteen years of Tory mis-rule' or 'Eight years of Labour mis-rule' or 'One week in politics is a long time at the end of the day' pale into insignificance beside Italy's 30 years or more of the Christian Democrats. The major fact about Italy is that, despite informed opinion that the country might actually operate better underwater, it is still there, visibly leaking but still afloat. It could, of course, be coming up for the third time. Quite frankly, though, I don't fancy going down four floors to revel in its former glories.

The Christian Democrats – something of a contradiction in terms, like Young Conservatives – came into being after World War II. The Italians had tried democracy before, after Italy's final unification in 1870 (achieved to the strains of the swinging mandolins of Garibaldi and his Red Shirts) but World War I so debilitated the country that by 1922 they'd got Mussolini in a big way.

Euro-fact: *Did you know that Mussolini was a Knight Commander of the Order of the Bath? This should give cause for pause to all those who returned their OBEs when the Beatles were elevated. And a few Bathers. It was given to him by a grateful George V.*

Never give a sucker an even break

Mussolini made the trains run on time, was given the Papal Seal of Approval in 1929, and then invaded Ethiopia, giving rise to Ethiopian jokes about castrati and ethnic junk necklaces. World War II was his Nemesis. Devoted though he was to Hitler, he wasn't that keen on entering the war. However, he did, then tried to get out of it. He was subsequently forced back in and was finally disposed of in the sort of circumstances that should discourage anyone from pursuing job satisfaction as a dictator – but never has.

A referendum was held and the populace settled this time for a republic. The Christian Democrat Party was created by the political arm of the Roman Catholic Church, and once more the Papal Seal of Approval was awarded. This was a considerable advantage since the second largest party in Italy is the Communist Party, which insists that it is not a communist party as in *the* Communist Party but simply *a* communist party and that it is eager to stick by the constitution and peacefully co-exist with the Christian Democrats in a coalition. However, when it comes to the ballot box, your average Italian is still torn asunder at the choice before him. On the one hand, there is the very corner-stone of democracy while on the other is the thought of excommunication, a chance to see

Dante's actual inferno, the wrath to come and the guilt, dear Lord, the guilt. Abandon hope, all ye who enter your 'X' against the Communist Party.

Why anyone should want to rule over the Italians, who are quite contentedly ungovernable, is another question, but the system at the moment calls for Dyno-rod, *the* drain-blasters. Most of the politicians are bent, and those that aren't dare not set foot outside for fear of being kidnapped or blown out of their trousers by terrorists. The Party is in the hands of men who have been there forever, and they spend most of their time sticking the traditional stiletto in each other's backs and ignoring the population totally. President Pertimi has been described as the 'freshest dash of youthful exuberance on the political scene' and *he's* 85. Italy is, quite frankly, a mess*. One of the main hazards of living in Rome nowadays is tripping over dead Libyans, but you're equally liable to be knee-capped by militant women. It comes as a great source of comfort to we Brits that, however low we sink in the Euro-pecking order, we are always one up on Italy, but it can't warm their Latin hearts. Italy is the only Euro-country with four active volcanoes. If it hadn't got them, it would probably have been awarded them, like red forks in the *Michelin Guide*.

I saw the Italian Foreign Minister, prior to the world summit in Venice, being questioned about the organisation. With intense pride, he replied: 'We had to do it from A to Zero'.

How To BE A SUCCESSFUL DICTATOR

RIGHT   WRONG

* **Fascinating Euro-gobbet:** *Prime Minister of Italy at the time of writing – and I only mention this because they tend to come and go like football managers – is Signor Francesco Cossiga. A Christian Democrat, actually, who was born in Sassari on the island of Sardinia. The leader of the Communist Party is Signor Enrico Berlingner who was born in Sassari on the island of Sardinia. The two men are cousins. In view of the particularly Italian attitude to the family, could this be the basis for a potential 800-page block-buster for Mario Puzo?*

In the FORUM, the daily queue forms of gentry eager to be Prime Minister for the day.

Sick as a Parrot

Such was the balls-aching nature of the European football championships in 1980 that, long after we have forgotten that Belgium reached the final – you see, you had forgotten already – the only scenes that will live in the memory are those on the terraces in Turin. The British are well to the fore in Euro-soccer hooliganism. Let us now praise famous men. Leeds United fans kicking the Parc des Princes to bits after losing the European Cup final. Glasgow Rangers' famous rape of Barcelona. Tottenham Hotspur's destruction of Rotterdam. And, after our failure to qualify for the World Cup finals in 1977, English fans picking up Luxembourg and throwing it a good foot east.

It came as no surprise, therefore, to read of the shock-horror 'I am ashamed to be an Englishman' furore that seized Turin when some British fans, quite properly you may think, cheerfully began to kick some old Belgians: in my view, a perfectly natural outlet for youthful exuberance. (Didn't we, before the war, pop over to Ostend and kick holes in their boaters and sand in their porky faces, after all?) This simple act of patriotism was rewarded with the most vicious police action. Those who thought the Italian police looked like the back row of the chorus in HMS Pinafore were amazed to see para-military thugs appear through the thick veil of tear-gas. They might well have surrendered. With Europe's television cameras upon them, of course, they must have been terrified of losing. It would have done the Italian image no good if their flak-jacketed, jack-booted Fuzz were seen to be driven out of the stadium by a jeering flock of English youths in vests.

Mrs Thatcher, then in Venice, instantly adopted Lord Carrington's firm and bold Death of a Princess posture and grovelled. England was let off with an £8,000 fine and a caution. The Italians became extravagantly self-righteous and, before the England-Italy game had begun, the referee had waved 803 red cards at the popular stand.

In Italy, football hooliganism is confined mainly to the home. This is quite sensible in that, in a local derby at the Olympic Stadium in Rome recently, a fan was killed with a maroon fired from the other side of the ground. Most fans at the ground are armed and, to some extent, armoured. A sensible precaution, but not that sensible, as an unfortunate woman in Genoa discovered when she switched over from the televised football to Cooking with Lucretia Borgia* or the like and was promptly shot dead by her husband. If Italy are playing, the vias empty but from every window you can hear whistling, horns blowing, and the eerie chorus of limbo that accompanies all continental soccer. If the Italians score, you're suddenly deafened by the roar of an empty street going mad. If the opposition score, move immediately to the middle of the road, as television sets are likely to rain down upon you from the windows above.

What rains down on your head when the entire local team is seized on the field and taken away in a police Ave Maria on a bribery and corruption rap, heaven alone dare guess.

> Q Why, you may enquire, don't they channel all the surplus energy engendered by the four volcanoes, the Sicilian brotherhood, the mama mia motherhood, their native passion and vigorous arm-waving?
>
> A Not a word, or they might.

* The Other Channel in Rome features hardish porn and is on offer to viewers after the late news. What price Body Fascism now? It's still more rewarding to sit in a dirty plastic mackintosh watching News at Ten with Anna Ford.

La Scala Violence

Anyone for Venice?

Can it really be more than 20 years since I was lured up the campanile of the church on the Isola di San Giorgio Maggiore by a mad monk? He seemed sane enough on the ground floor: a holy man, given to a life of prayer and chastity, with a day-job as a lift-attendant. He very slowly filled his lift and, on what seemed like the third day, we ascended. He released us into the most delightful open-air belfry with stunning views of Venice and the Lido and beyond. We wandered about enjoying the view and inspecting the vast bells immediately above us. He waited by the lift. Of a sudden, the bells struck up. The bells! The bells! I understood the phrase 'like the clappers' at once: it was instant shell-shock. It was Blondel being thrown down Ben Nevis in a dustbin full of alarm-clocks and saucepans – a feat I realise he never undertook. No fool, Blondel! Clutching our ears, we all staggered back to the lift. With a laugh that was lost in the awesome cacophony the Mad Monk leapt into his lift and headed downwards, leaving his deafened flock beating on the gates or feverishly pressing at the buzzer. I still scream when a clock chimes.

It's a strange thing but, while I still remember the pigeons, the rival orchestras around the Piazza San Marco, and the Bridge of Sighs, what's stuck most firmly in my mind is the bad language I heard in Italy. I once sat behind two Venetians in a water-bus and found, with a sense of intense pride, that their incomprehensible Italian was interspersed with the finest of Anglo-Saxon four-letter words. It was like reading the Chinese *Lady Chatterley* where, in the midst of otherwise meaningless but pretty text, all the racy bits are in English.

And again, I was sitting in a restaurant, having a beer and revelling in Italian body language, when I observed a cardinal and a layman at another table. The soup arrived; I think they just dip the bowls in the canal and heat the contents. It was thick with creatures.

The cardinal made to mutter an amazing grace over the steaming dishes. The layman, clearly a crawler and possibly related to some of the soup, silenced him with a lifted palm. He then proceeded to rattle off a stream of Latin, obviously to impress the man of God, who looked extremely bored. After what seemed an eternity, the unctuous layman concluded his devotions, raised a large spoonful of soup to his smirking lips, drank deep, screamed, and spat the contents over both table and cardinal, mouthing as he did so some of the vilest language I've never understood a word of.

Strange, but even as I write, I can hear Tories in the street outside, shouting, in the true spirit of the Common Market: 'Buy British!' Great.

TERRORISMO

In 1979 there were 2,514 terrorist incidents in Italy, responsibility for which was spread over 147 different terrorist organisations. Mr Cossiga, the current Prime Minister, has just avoided impeachment on a charge of helping the son of one of his colleagues to escape police clutches. The lad is but one of 41 sons, daughters, nephews, nieces, uncles and aunts of senior politicians wanted by the police on terrorism raps. *O tempora! O morons!*

DENMARK

First up, I'd better confess that I've never been to Denmark. When I was about 10 years old I was at school with a Dane who taught me the Danish word for some sort of native rice pudding. The pronunciation can only be mastered by a trained Dane, apparently, containing as it does a number of hawking noises and guttural sounds pitched too low for the human ear. The basic effect was 'Erck-merk-fallerkport'. Those 'k's are where the problems arise: the Danes are also famous for their glottal stop. As a fund of information it doesn't add up to much, though.

In my experience, the thing to do at this juncture is to write 'Denmark' on a large piece of paper and walk around it until inspiration strikes. Ha! Twice round, and into my brain leapt hard porn and Lego. Very Danish. Hence the phrase 'getting your lego over'. There's also bacon, butter, blue cheese, blue movies, *I am Curious, Blue* (the life of an inquisitive Australian?), Hans Andersen, the Tivoli Gardens (Herbert Morrison's inspiration for the Battersea Fun Fair), the royal family on bicycles, and a mermaid whose head is sawn off occasionally as a protest against what I cannot imagine. Free Heligoland? Free Legoland? And there's Copenhagen, of course, described by Frank Loesser in his film *Hans Christian*

Andersen as the 'salty old queen of the sea'. Hello, sailor!

In addition, there's Carlsberg, Tuborg and Hamlet the gloomy Dane, pillage, rape and, to some extent, Magnus Magnusson though the Icelandic connection was severed in 1944.

Lars Tuborg Rape and Pillage in the Newcastle Area

Amazing Eurofact unknown to me until I purchased a huge, boring map of the community: *Did you know that Greenland was in the EEC? Did you realise that we can go to Greenland and do freely and without let or hindrance whatsoever may be the current whim, fancy or elephantine caprice of the powers-that-are in Brussels? Since 1953, Greenland has been a county of Denmark. What a crafty ruse! Why doesn't New Zealand become a Riding of Yorkshire? Or part of the Midlands? This would bring an immediate end to all the invidious sheepmeat business in one bold stroke. Incidentally and en passant – my word, this is a fascinating book – did you know that Old Zealand was Denmark's largest island?*

Greenland was named by Eric the Red when discovered by the Vikings in 900. As it clearly is not at all green, one can only assume that Eric was colour-blind. In which case, was he Eric the Mauve?

HANS CHRISTIAN ANDERSEN

You can forget *The Red Shoes, The Princess and The Pea* and *The Ugly Duckling*. Were you aware that Hans Andersen's first roaring success was a book called *A Journey on Foot from Holman's Canal to the East Point of Amager?* I like a title that tells you what the book is all about but is it wise, as Hans Christian does here, to give away the ending? Agatha Christie would have kicked herself if she'd called her play *The Mousetrap – The Policeman Did It.**

*(*Her play, of course, gets its first mention in Hamlet:*
King: *What do you call the play?*
Hamlet: *The Mousetrap. Marry, how? Tropically.*
(That dates it.)

There is a famous old Danish proverb that runs: 'The pig hangs on the cow's tail'. This is not, as you might think, an interesting insight into Danish police methods, but is based on the sound Danish agricultural policy of feeding the pigs skim-milk. Is this the sort of romanticism you've been looking for, the uplifting hoist you've been hoping for from the Great Thing?

I remember Lord Longford went to Copenhagen on displeasure bent, though what *he* was searching for I'm not certain. He was then chairman of, unless memory has played strange tricks, the Royal Commission on Filth and Smut. He went to a live sex show in our interests, and walked out before the big number, never to know to what depths of depravity or corruption he might have or might not have sunk.

Q How gloomy are Danes?

A I've no idea and I only have my friend with the glottal stop and Hamlet, Prince of Denmark, as any sort of guide. 'Glottal Stop' was given to moments of depression, and Hamlet borders on the manic, but this is probably because he's never been played by a comedian. Elsinore Castle is a gloomy place, at best, permanently under thick fog and bags of dry ice. The grave-diggers seem very gay, though.

THE NETHERLANDS

If you think the Germans can eat, then, upon my word, you should watch a gang of Dutchpersons in action. In Amsterdam, for instance, should there be a mild rumbling in the stomach between the 12-course lunch and the traditional 93-course Reystafel dinner (a never-ending series of Indonesian dishes), many street corners sport 24-hour vending machines which provide such snacks as eggs, bacon and double chips to ease the pangs.

I was sitting quietly the other day in the local curry-house, having a re-think on reincarnation and waiting for an explosive take-away, when a bus-load of Hollanders entered. There must have been 10 or so couples; all burly folk, and all clearly eager for the trough. Their tour-guide took charge. Without consultation, he automatically ordered mixed grills for all, then they all settled down to study the menu. They selected prawn dansak, a meal in itself, for starters. 'Vegetable pilau with the mixed grills', they demanded. The waiter explained helpfully that these, like the dansaks, came with their own rice. '*Extra* rice all round then', said the tour-guide. 'Are there potatoes with the vegetable pilau?' someone enquired. 'Some', said the waiter. 'More boiled potatoes', pronounced their leader, scanning the congregation, 'all round'. They were already

The Sheer Excitement of Being European.
Dutch people waiting for Dinner.

averaging 3.75 lesser mortals' meals each and the night was young. I left with my modest take-away, wondering how the EEC can run up surplusses. This lot would have reduced the butter mountain to a rancid molehill in no time.

As I walked home, I decided that no country than can produce Rembrandt can be all bad, but then again, no country than can come up with the Boers can be entirely good, either. To give the Dutch their due, however, they seem more pleasant in the northern hemisphere but then I'm not black, though I do have a lively sense of rhythm and a definite weakness outside the off-stump. Nor am I a Moluccan.

I first visited Amsterdam in 1957, and it was only as the train approached the German/Dutch border that it flashed through my brain that I had not an inkling of what the Dutch spoke – either how it sounded or how it looked. There is the ancient theory that most foreigners will respond to English if it's shouted slowly, but I've found over the years that the language of signs, coupled with farmyard impressions – a sort of Percy Edwards for the hard of hearing – is quite the most satisfactory method. In the corridor of a train travelling from Zagreb to Athens I once found myself next to a Yugoslav house-painter. We conducted a lively 12-hour conversation which consisted entirely of a combination of sign-language, six words of German that we shared from various military occupations and crude pictures drawn on a steamy window. I don't think Parkinson or Robin Day could have elicited more information from my friend, had he been blessed with English as his first language, and indeed the interview would have been infinitely less entertaining visually.

But what about the Dutch? And how did the phrase 'double-Dutch' ever ease its way into common parlance? In fact, I was to discover that this is an ordinary measure of Bols' Navy Blue Gin but, as I walked from the station in search of a bed, I was an innocent abroad. I spotted a pleasing-looking pub overlooking a canal and, realising that I could at least say 'Heineken!', I entered, said 'Heineken!' and there I was with a beer. I then pondered on my next question, and watched two gentlemen playing billiards at a table without pockets, which seemed a pointless exercise at best. I realised that if I said 'Bed?' in a guttural, Germanic sort of way,

The Old Edam Emptying

anything could happen. I remember Hamburg, even if you don't. I also remember being told by a fellow-actor of an alarming incident in a Spanish restaurant. It was his first visit to Spain but, proud of his smattering of their tongue, he set about ordering in a loud, clear voice. The waiter collapsed into hysterical laughter, and was quick to spread the gaiety among his colleagues and the clientele. I won't describe the mime to you, but it was explained finally to the bewildered thespian that he had demanded oral sex and chips.

I approached mine host, a cheerful-looking barrel of a man. 'Engelhish?' I enquired, in a querulous do-it-yourself Esperanto. 'Sure!' he replied, in broad American. 'Hell, I came up through France with the Sixth Army.' He spoke

better American that I did. I found this pretty
general. (You'll say that there's no such thing as
a pretty general but, *chacun à son goût,* you're
the sort of person who shouldn't be allowed
near a book.)

I like the Dutch. There, I've said it. They take
their pleasures cheerfully. They smile
contentedly over their huge dinners, the ladies
of the night beam happily from their windows,
and they drink more than merrily. What they
drink is pretty weird, however. Bols gin tastes
like paint-stripper. (I was about to say
'furniture-remover' but I've never got my teeth
into a Pickford.) My first Bols was the most
disgusting drink I've ever sipped. The second
wasn't much better, but the third, strangely
enough, seemed quite acceptable. I brought
some home in a brown, earthenware bottle but I
could never steel myself to partake of that first
drink and I threw the bottle away, unopened, 20
years later. Like Pernod and Gauloise
cigarettes, Bols gin is best taken *in situ.* Ouzo is
the same: you need Greece about you when
indulging.

For an interesting drinking experience,
cross the square opposite the Royal Palace in
Amsterdam and set off down a long thin street
which, if relatively sober, you can't miss.
Halfway down on the left is a small bar run by a
school-mistress of some age, or so it seems.
The rules are made clear from a wall-full of
cartoons. The licensees are the charmingly-
named firm of Weinand Focking (a
contradiction in terms if ever there was one).
The rules of the house are as follows. Firstly,
select your poison from the bottles arrayed
behind Miss Buss or Miss Beale – I recommend
half-and-half, which is half curaçao, I think, and
the other half is lost in the mists of the first half.
Madame will then fill a wine glass to the brim
and place it in front of you on the scrubbed
bar-top. Everything in Holland is scrubbed

Mata Hari
Seen here on the *qui-vive* for a Marshal Foch. (A rude
readers writes 'A martial what?') She was born in Holland,
worked for the Germans, and was shot by the French. A
true European!

clean: the people, the windmills, the beds, and the bar-tops. As spilling is ruled out, following the instructions on the wall, the customer must place his hands behind his back and, stooping to the glass, take a sip. Half-and-half produces instant pain between the eyes but, oh, it eases.

Another delight for the tourist is the porno museum, if it's still there. It was in danger of falling into a canal when I visited it. There are those who may say that I seem to dwell over-heavily on the seamier side of the continent, but I find it casts interesting side-lights on the varying national attitudes of our European colleagues. Heaven knows, we British are grand at trooping the colour and celebrating the Queen Mother's 80th birthday, but our seamy side is extravagantly vile. However, the porno museum is, or was, a joyous celebration. A wonderfully rude and funny version of *Snow White and the Seven Dwarfs* greeted one. It could have come from the Disney studio itself. No, it couldn't. There was also a hilarious guide to contraceptive devices through the ages, which were presented in glass cases with all the solemnity of Roman left-overs.

As I said, no country that can come up with Rembrandt, not to mention Vincent van Gogh, can be all bad. These are the only two artists, in my view, ever to be captured realistically on celluloid. Rembrandt (the best) was played by Charles Laughton and Vincent by Kirk Douglas. I couldn't believe in Anthony Quinn's Gauguin. I felt the only thing he could have successfully

The Dutch royals, Beatrix and Claus, seen here on the night of their coronation, about to move into the traditional Dutch squat.

put on canvas would have been a punch-drunk light heavyweight. And God help the Tahitian lovelies over 15 rounds.

LUXEMBOURG

What can one say about Luxembourg that hasn't already been said, and to my certain knowledge no one has mentioned it. I used to listen to Luxembourg in the days when wirelesses were wirelesses and the romantically dialled, far-away places with strange-sounding names like Heligoland and Droitwich were painted thereon. It was more sensible too; you knew where you were with the Home Service and the Light Programme. I've now lost the BBC entirely, but the German Third Programme comes through clear as a bell. This is presumably the old Lord Haw-Haw wave-band. He always did sound a deal clearer than Uncle Mac.

Radio Luxembourg was quite racy in those days, and the commercials seemed extremely exciting to our untutored ears. When asked the hour, I still find myself saying 'The time by my H. Samuel Ever-rite is . . .' to baffled listeners, whom I then further mystify by slowly fading into total silence which used, I recall, to be Radio Luxembourg's trade-mark at like moments of truth.

What little information I have been able to garner re Luxembourg comes from a brochure advertising its Holiday Inn, and it seems to say it all in four languages. The hotel is apparently situated 'in the heart of the European Centre', or 'au cœur du Centre Européen' if you prefer, or

indeed – God, it's an ugly language – 'im Herzen des Europäischen Zentiums'. It is also, according to the brochure, 'en la Koro de la eŭropaj institucioj'. Yes, fans, it's Esperanto! The Esperantos reckon that their moment of glory has come, for Luxembourg is one of the seats of the European Parliament and they consider that they may well have the solution to the language problem. The nine member countries have six working languages: English, French, German, Italian, Dutch and Danish. Thus in Parliament each language has its box which is geared to interpreting the other five languages at any one time, or all at once in the case of a shouting-match or unseemly heckling. The Tower of Babel will seem like a Trappist building-site when the Greeks, the Spanish and the Portuguese sign on.

Interpreting, of course, is not only a full-time occupation at the European Parliament. Sixty per cent of the Parliamentary budget goes on translation, which the *Daily Express* has reduced to the simpler statistic of Euro-MPs talking at £10 per word. There are, of course, innumerable meetings, gatherings, off-the-record discussions and, most formidable of all, the paper mountain.

A German commissioner sends a memorandum to a French commissioner, and casually moots copies to the other seven, and paper proliferates in a multitude of tongues. I've seen pictures of the girls working at a revolving table piled high with foolscap, shuffling and dealing like the Cincinnati Kid at 78 rpm. And *I* worry about the forests of the world when I throw away a paper bag.

Picture the scene when a Danish bureaucrat seeks to explain the intricacies of building an abattoir in Lego to a Portuguese. A German interpreter may volunteer to translate from the Danish into German, which a French interpreter with a smattering of Italian can pass on to a Portuguese interpreter with a dash of Latin. So much for the art of conversation.

It has been suggested that the whole beastly business might be conducted in French and English. However, this practical thought (actually, they could drop the French) is greeted by fellow-Europeans with a volley of abuse in Danish, Walloon, Erse, Italian, Dutch, and the hideous sound of peeved Kraut. No small wonder that the Esperanto-wallahs think they're onto a good thing.

Here is a plug for their songbooks, available from the Esperanto-Asocio de Britujo.

All together now!

```
Kantoj    Songbooks                                                          1.25
BEA Kantokolekto, 73 kantoj kun melodioj kaj akordoj en plasta kovrilo.  (po 10) 0.15
BEA Kantfolioj, N-ro 3  ..  ..  ..  ..  ..  ..  ..  ..  ..  ..  ..  ..  ..        0.85
Dum la noktoj - Auld kaj aliaj - kantlibro kun melodioj  ..  ..  ..  ..  ..      0.75
Fioroj sen kompar' - Hill/Auld - kun meliodoj kaj akordoj .  ..  ..  ..  ..  ..  0.75
   antanta mia bird' -      "        "        "       "    ..  ..  ..  ..  ..    0.25
Kantante tra Pollando - 23 kantoj - vortoj kaj muziko  ..  ..  ..  ..  ..  ..
```

Luxembourg is where all the vital EEC documents are kept. Thus, when the Euro-Parliament has its monthly in Strasbourg*, the juggernauts are mustered and great containers stuffed with words rumble off, followed by the requisite thousand or so civil servants, freeloaders and carpetbaggers to a person. After a week the caravan returns. On occasion, it packs up and heads for Brussels. This costs us all about £10 million a year.

In a building not unlike one of those sophisticated containers designed for the car roof.

Fascinating Euro-fact: *Erse is an official language of the EEC. There is one copy of the* Treaty of Rome *in Erse, which is a longer, infinitely duller, and far more expensive work than* The Book of Kells *and, I would have thought, a contender for the* Record Book of Guinnesses.

EURO-DISEASES

A doctor writes: There's no doubt that, on the continent, you can contract some pretty vile diseases, quite apart from the traditional ones. Heaven knows, I've been warning my patients for years now about the perils of Johnny Syphilis and Clarence Clap, as I refer to them jocularly. I also make certain where I can that my patients take a hamper full of binding medicaments because, quite honestly, nothing puts more of a damper on one's vacation than spending the 14 days staggering from one's bed to the, let's face it, rather primitive toilet facilities one finds there. Donald Diarrhoea comes along in many guises. I recommend that you don't drink any water and avoid all fish-food. 'See Naples and die of botulism!' is one crack we medicos have certainly enjoyed over the years, and I thoroughly relished this quip from a colleague:

'Went on a fishing-trip in Tuscany last year and all we caught was salmonella!' How we roared!

There's every chance, of course, that you'll be as sick as a cat if you travel over there by hovercraft or ferry. Air-sickness can also undo you in no uncertain manner. Make sure you're fully insured against any unpleasantness that may overtake you: a sudden hernia while lifting your duty-free goods, or the morning dive into an unfinished swimming-pool. Make certain you have the addresses of British hospitals where available. When in doubt, fly home.

Should you fall under the spell of some foreigner – and I know we all like to let our hair down on holiday – and it comes to Freddie Fornication*, don't dally but head straight to the bathroom for a really good scrub and a hypodermic full of penicillin. Better safe than

International hospitals in Europe

France

American Hospital,
63 Bd Victor-Hugo, Neuilly
(Near Paris)
Telephone MAI 6800

British Hospital (Hertford)
48 R. de Villiers, Levallois
Telephone: PER 3320

British American Hospital,
31-33 Blvd Maeterlinck, Nice,
Alps Maritimes
Telephone: 855327-855359

Spain

British American Hospital,
Calle Limite 1, Madrid
Telephone: 23456700

Italy

American Medical Center,
Via Ludovisi 36, Rome
Telephone: 464 143-485 706

There is no equivalent international hospital in Germany, but more hospitals there have English-speaking staff.

scrofulous. How true that old adage is today!** Have yourself thoroughly injected before you leave. I do a jolly useful little package that should protect you against the worst excesses of cholera, Black Death, bubonic plague, rat bites, German measles, Dutch elm disease, a Frog in the throat, a toad in the hole or meeting a Belgian. Have a happy holiday!

---

* Beware of that seemingly innocent and oh-so-enjoyable nibble of your ear-lobe. Rabies is ever-rampant over there. The Channel's not there for nothing!

** I caught a very nasty dose in Lourdes. What an irony, eh?

I haf come for mein Rabies shot

Gilbert's Black Death is still playing him up rotten.

THE END

'If the debate is to come alive, what is really needed is a book which describes the *experience* as well as the structure of membership of the Community. The EEC may not be sexy, but it needs a Gay Talese': *The Times* (25 July 1980)

God knows, I've tried to describe the experience but, when I compare the energy expended to encourage the Childe Rushton to think British with like attempts to encourage my Europeanism, there's no comparison. I can't go along with the 'Great Thing outside the living room' theory and I can't blindly follow those who support the Euro-notion regardless because they like Wagner and because the food's better over there. And with Portugal, Spain and Greece to come, just how European do we have to be?

I can hear the Euro-heckle already: have you no vision? Can you not see beyond the butter mountain where sheepmeat may safely graze? Somewhere over the rainbow, you hairy-faced rabble-rouser, bluebirds sing! They may well, I reply, but I can't hear the bustards. All I can hear is the cry of the cuckoo. And it's never good news. A possible exception, I suppose, is if you're unemployed. Given Mother Thatcher's sympathetic suggestion that you should move house, and the freedom of movement within the Market, you could go and be unemployed in Italy instead*. Otherwise, it's hardly soul-stirring stuff that emerges from Brussels. For example, there's alarmist dicta about our sausages, ice-cream, beer and taxis being 'brought into line', the abolition of the British milkman, the introduction of cardboard milk in plastic containers, the number of peas in a Euro-pod, tachometers and juggernauts, and the compulsory Euro-handshake, so that everything will be identical and 'Foreign muck!' will no longer reverberate throughout our green and pleasant land.

The fishermen of England have had it, metrication was a monster con and, since Peter Walker surrendered the Green Pound, the old cheap food policy is a thing of the past. Given Europe's firm stands on, for instance, whether or not to take the cruise missile or boycott the Olympics, the thought of monetary union should cause a larger flutter in the City than the death of a royal corgi.

And another. The EEC now offers subsidies to farmers to grow cannabis of about £3.69 per hundredweight above the market price.

Rise above all this, cry the Euros, these are but early days and growing pains. Europeans don't care who's in charge – presidents, dictators or coalitions – as long as they can stroll abroad of a summer evening, fat wife in one hand and the legs of a kicking chicken in the other, while gobbing onto the pavement at every other step. We do. Well, all right, not that much but it would be good to retain the option.

When you read of three Australian kids falling over a £50,000 nugget north of Melbourne, you can rely on that being the sort of place with a future for generations to come. You won't find much joy under the ground in Europe with a metal-detector, except bits of previous Europes. Europe does great ruins and, indeed, potential ruins, and is high on pomp and circumstance and old masters and dead languages and, all in all, could be the museum of the century. As anything more, alas, the world's largest multi-national conglomerate is a continental dog's breakfast.